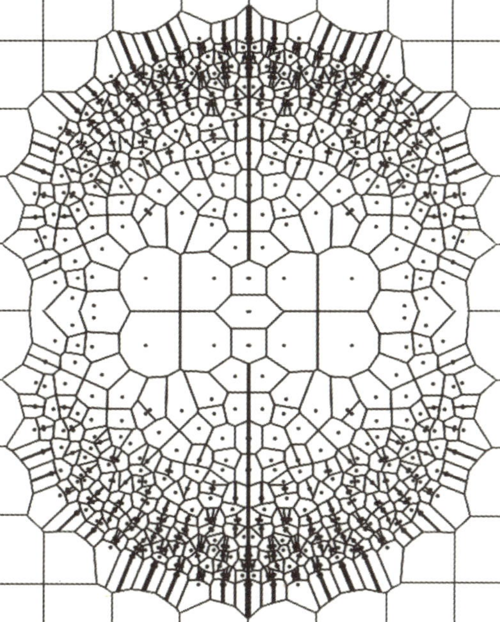

ANARCHY IN THE ORGANISM

ANARCHY IN THE ORGANISM

Simeon Nelson

black dog publishing

ANARCHY IN THE ORGANISM (CANCER AS A COMPLEX SYSTEM)

Artist Residency at the UCH Macmillan Cancer Centre, London, January 2011–April 2012.
Installation in the Capper Street windows of the UCLH Macmillan Cancer Centre, London April 2012–July 2013.
Live performance at the John Lill Music Centre, University of Hertfordshire with Kate Romano on clarinet, 15 May 2012.
Symposium at the Wellcome Collection Conference Centre, London, 22 June 2012.

Technical Data
4 Samsung UE55D8000YU video monitors.
4 SumVision Cyclone micro 2+ media players.
4 Samson Servo 200 power amplifiers.
8 Feonic F4PRO Audio drive transducers.
8 laser-cut vinyl patterns applied to inside glazing surfaces and back surfaces of window cavities.

Artist: Simeon Nelson.
Software: Nick Rothwell.
Music: Rob Godman.
Consulting Scientist: Simon Walker-Samuel.
Curator: Guy Noble.
Patient Representative: Gilly Angell.

Commissioned by UCLH Arts.
Supported by the Wellcome Trust.
anarchyintheorganism.tumblr.com.
http://simeon-nelson.com/index.php/anarchy-in-the-organism/

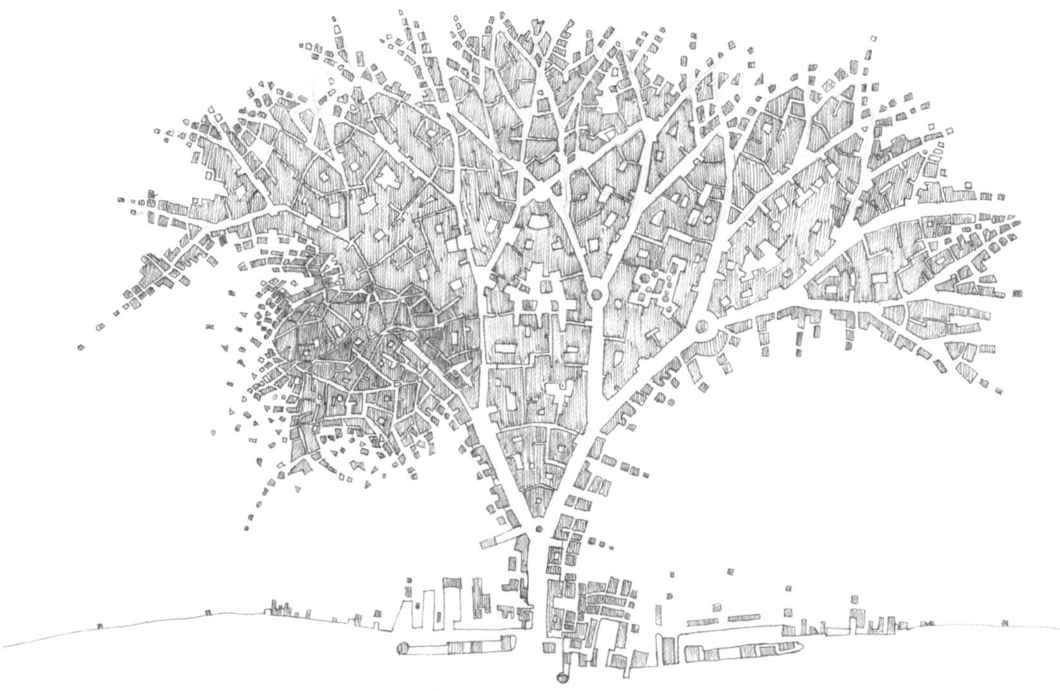

Oncoburg, pen on A3 paper, Simeon Nelson, 2012. Drawing using cartographic conventions to draw analogies between organic and urban growth patterns.

Artist's sketch of urban expansion, which was interpreted by an oncologist as a representation of tumour growth.

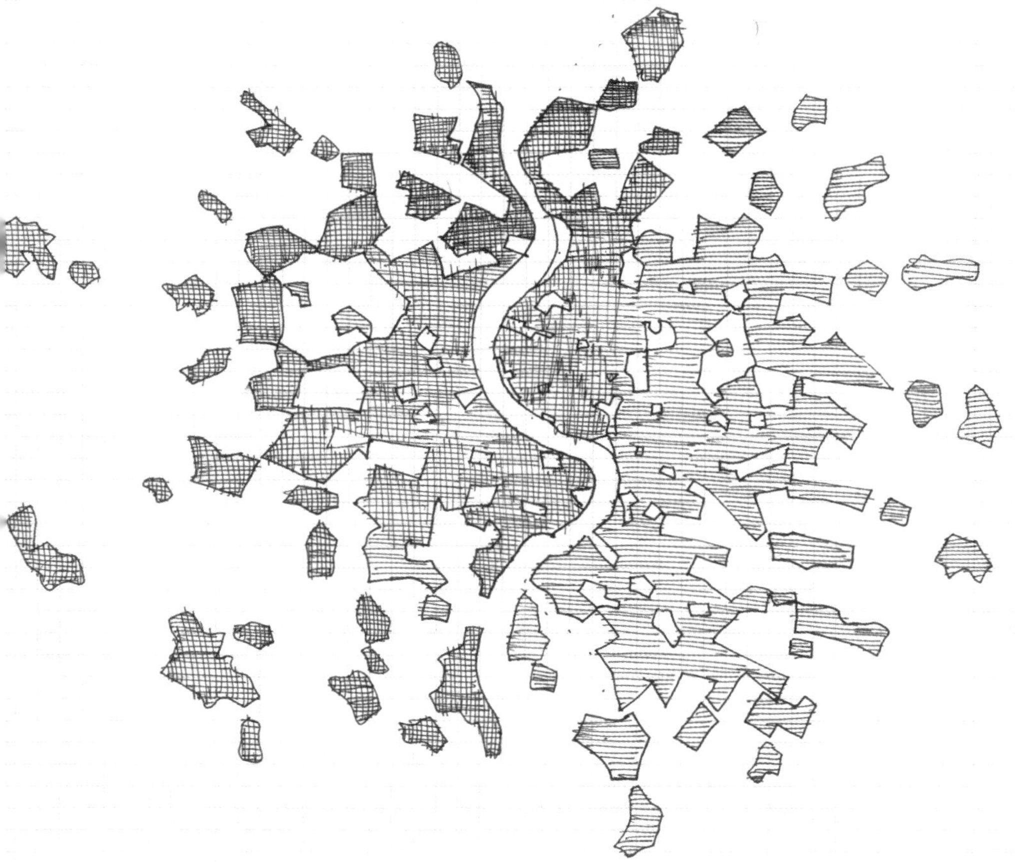

AN ARTIST RESIDENCY AT UCH MACMILLAN CANCER CENTRE

Guy Noble

The starting point for any art commission within a healthcare space is the patient themselves. It is my role as Arts Curator of University College London Hospital NHS Foundation Trust to understand the patients' health needs and their emotional state of mind when visiting the hospital, and to communicate this to the artist. Patients are not your average gallery-going public. The general public make an active choice about visiting a gallery or museum. Once patients, however, they have little choice about visiting a hospital and engaging with the art within. This is something I always have to be sensitive to when commissioning art at UCH and was one of the challenges facing Simeon Nelson in his 18-month residency at University College Hospital Macmillan Cancer Centre. This introduction will provide some context to his residency, positioning it in the tradition of arts in health work and highlighting some of the challenges of working in such an emotionally charged environment.

Artist residencies within hospitals are not unusual and art's relationship to healthcare can be traced back to ancient Greece and specifically the town of Epidaurus, to which people from all over Greece flocked to visit the Temple of Asklepios, the god of healing. As part of the healing process they were prescribed walks to "the amphitheatre (which is still in use today) to attend performances of tragedies or comedies".[1]

1. Senior, P and J Croall, *Helping to Heal: The Arts in Health Care*, Calouste Gulbenkian Foundation, 1993, p. 3.

Over the last 30 years there has been a proliferation of arts in health activity and many hospitals have commissioned artists to create work for the benefit of the patients that they serve. Interestingly, from the Medieval period art played a part in communicating the message of care and comfort through spiritual depictions of the afflicted, sick and dying being attended to by saints.

The Cancer Centre was open to the pubic in April 2012 and is an outpatient facility that addresses the treatment needs for cancer patients in the twenty-first century, with individual floors tailored to the investigation and treatment of specific cancers. UCLH Arts, the arts programme that serves UCLH NHS Foundation Trust, commissioned artists to create artworks throughout the building that not only reflect the kind of first-class quality care that patients will receive there, but also to provide patients and visitors with an uplifting environment which encourages engagement with and conversations around the artworks.

As an artist who works with ideas such as complexity theory, cybernetics and the philosophy of science, Simeon Nelson is fascinated with the

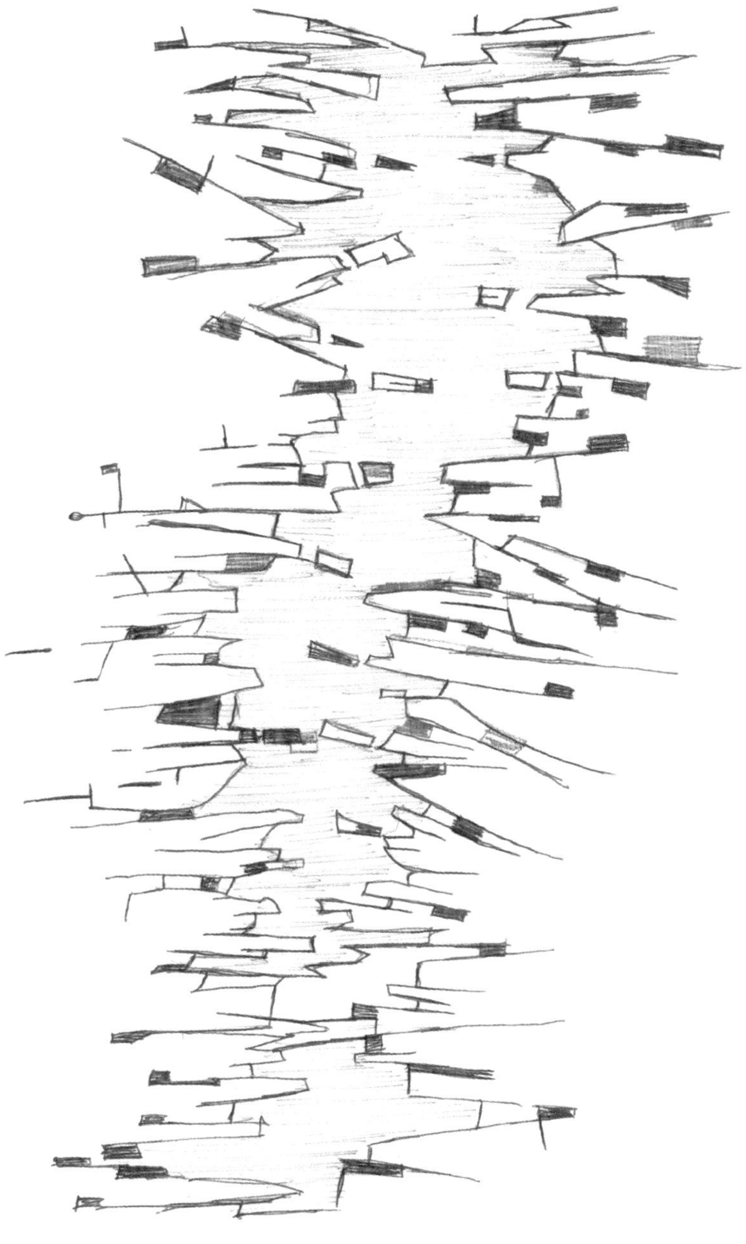

biology of the human body, how it assembles itself into a complex organism and how we maintain a sense of self within the growing and aging process. Nelson's interest in the impact of visualisation on public

ABOVE *Oncogenetic Landscape*, pen on A3 paper, Simeon Nelson, 2011. Response to a cancer patient's description of severe mandibular nerve-pain in an interview in June 2011 in studio.

understanding of science can be seen in his past work, as demonstrated in his use of popular and iconic images from the history of science—such as the Bohr atom—and Haeckel's Darwinian Tree of Life. His ability to create meaningful and engaging visual imagery, combined with a rigorous and reflective approach, made him an ideal choice to be an artist in residence at the Centre.

Nelson distilled his initial thinking for the residency into the following operative metaphors and concepts:

- Control/anarchy.
- Autopoeisis (literally 'self-production').
- Cancer as a complex system nested within the body and societal system.

The key objectives within the residency were to:

- Engage patients, visitors, staff and the public with the science of cancer and its social, cultural and ethical impact.
- Produce an artwork based on current research into cancer as a complex system.
- Contribute to the public understanding of cancer through the artwork, public fora, and a publication discussing cancer in a social and cultural context.

Nelson worked closely with researchers, patients and staff, interviewing them on personal, emotional, social, cultural and scientific aspects of cancer. These conversations formed the foundations for the final commission and in the process threw up challenges for Nelson around notions of autonomy and the responsibility of the artist to the viewer or, in this case, the patient. Early research and sketches compared metastasising cancer to the urban growth of a city, which resulted in strong negative reactions from some patients. In an environment where patients already feel dehumanised by the clinical procedures they endure, it is vital from a curatorial point of view that the art does not accentuate the feeling of alienation. Nelson readily admits that he was far more comfortable dealing with the scientific aspect of cancer both emotionally and intellectually; but to his credit he re-evaluated his work and persevered, keeping an open dialogue with patients about the development of the project. I believe this readiness to engage with patients provided a vital link between the science of cancer and the care of patients, who so often feel far removed from the treatment process.

Nelson also worked closely with Simon Walker-Samuel, Senior Research Associate at the UCL Centre for Advanced Biomedical Imaging, to generate computer code based on Voronoi cells to simulate cancer life and death. Combining this with input from patients and a soundscape by composer Rob Godman, he created a digital artwork depicting organisms in different states of growth, mutation and decay as a normal aspect of being alive. The work, displayed over four screens, housed within street facing windows on Capper Street, are each surrounded with a vinyl concentric design very much in Nelson's sculptural style. As in life, the images portraying cancer that evolve from the computer code do so randomly, sometimes displaying cancer cells developing and sometimes not. Sometimes showing the cancer cells and non-cancer cells co-existing and, at other times, depicting the cancer cells taking over the entire system. To have this work so honestly portraying the processes of cancer within a dedicated centre such as this is brave and without doubt challenging. However, it is refreshing in that it does not seek to patronise the audience by giving a sugar-coated view of life; it allows the viewer space to reflect on different scenarios of it. Nelson succeeded in the residency as he was able to translate and visualise the science of cancer by placing the disease within the context of the patient. Through interviewing and using patient stories to provide an emotional—and therefore human—narrative to the science, he created something that is haunting but ultimately beautiful.

Gilly Angell, a patient and contributor to this book agrees: "Simeon's piece demonstrates, at times, a very challenging collaboration between patients and the artist, of how art and by

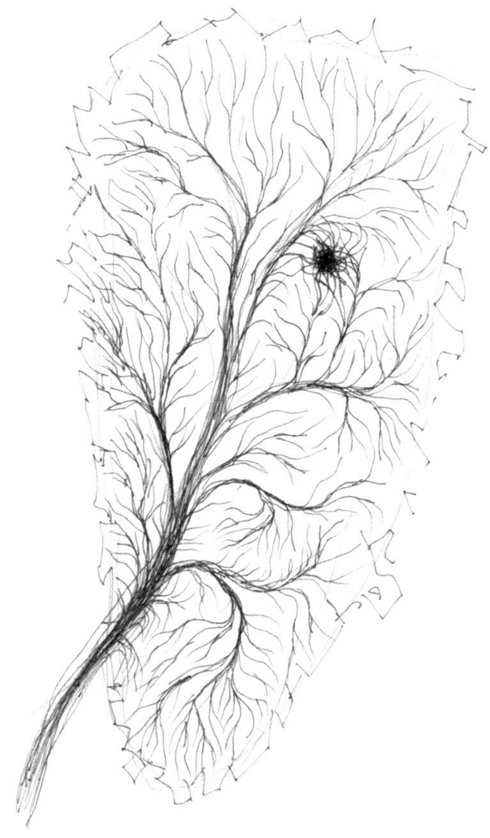

ABOVE *Oncogenetic Landscape*, pen on A3 paper, Simeon Nelson, 2012. Based on the description of a lung tumour by a cancer patient.

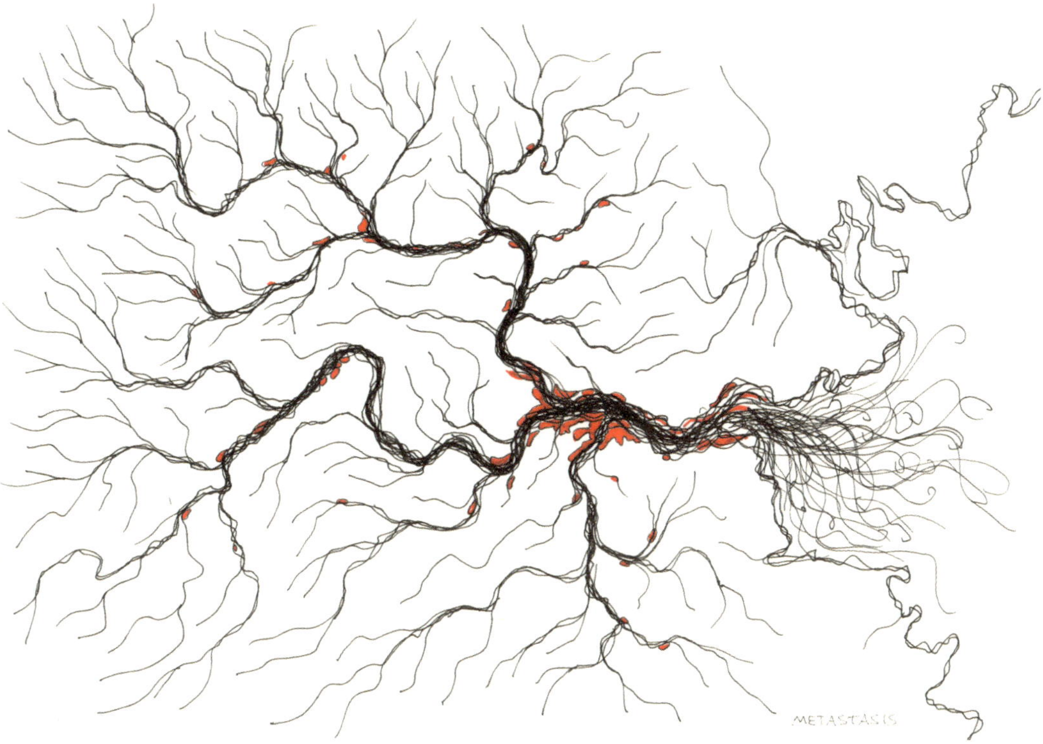

definition an artist can represent something as personal as cancer, that the commission, like the initial diagnosis of the cancer, is a process, a journey which eventually has evolved into a piece with inherent sacred beauty."[2]

2. Angell, G, Personal Correspondence with Arts Curator, 2012.

ABOVE *Oncogenetic Landscape*, pen on A3 paper, Simeon Nelson, 2011.

A VIEW FROM THE OTHER SIDE: A PATIENT PERSPECTIVE

Gilly Angell

Dance when you are broken open.
Dance, if you have torn your bandage off.
Dance in the middle of fighting.
Dance in your blood.
Dance when you are perfectly free.[1]

1. Rumi, Jelaluddin, *The Essential Rumi*, C Barks and J Moyne trans., San Francisco: HarperCollins USA, 1996, p. 281.

I would like to thank the Wellcome Trust for funding this art commission whose aim is to stimulate interest, excitement and debate about bio medical sciences through the arts.

I have been involved from the beginning of this project, as a Patient Representative of the UCLH Arts and Heritage Committee, and have seen this piece initiate intense debate.

A third of this commission is about the patient perspective of cancer, which in turn allows scientists and doctors to begin to understand the complex, many-layered journey that each and every one of us who has had a cancer diagnosis undertakes.

No-one can share another's cancer. I own my cancer completely. Others can share in another's cancer journey as a witness in the roles of clinician, scientist, family, friends and artist.

When you have experienced any cancer, you hold emotional, psychological, mental and spiritual resonances deep within your cellular memory.

In any cancer diagnosis there are three perspectives: the clinician, the scientist (who, for the patient, is the unseen partner) and the patient. All too often the experience of the patient is sidelined—not intentionally. My experience of cancer is not just biochemical. It is the sum of my emotional journey, an investment that can be transformed into a profound other worldly experience that is self-nurturing.

On seeing Simeon's first drawings for the installation I was horrified. Or in the words of Guy Noble, Arts Curator and David Wherritt, Chair of the Arts Committee: "You were so angry." It took me quite a while to understand why I had had such a visceral reaction to the piece.

The seventeenth century philosopher John Locke stated that personal identity was dependent on autobiographical, pre-episodic memories: i.e., that we are all the sum total of our memories. Therefore, my pre-cancer and cancer memories informed my perception of the artwork, an artwork which at its very heart externalised a very internal process that I, and anyone who has had cancer, have experienced at a cellular level—cells multiplying out of control. I had lived and witnessed my cancer take my body to the brink of destruction, on life support. As time went by a number of questions began to coalesce.

Did I wish to see cancer depicted in art? Many years ago I had walked out of a Damien Hirst exhibition at the White Cube where he had shown blown-up images (12 metres by 12 metres) of the blood films of his mother's cancer. So, my initial reaction to Simeon's work was not just, because I had had cancer.

Could any artist, unless they had undergone a cancer diagnosis, depict cancer artistically?

But then is that not the role of the artist?—To depict a subject that challenges us, that maybe we as non-artists do not have the visual language to depict?

There was something more. It was then that I realised what the initial piece did not reflect.

Even in the darkest and longest nights of the soul I had experienced over and over again profound periods of peace, serenity, beauty and of just being.

That is not captured down a microscope. Or is it?

A few weeks ago I saw for the first time, courtesy of Professor Paul Moss of Birmingham University and Dr Emma Morris—who was part of my brilliant transplant team at UCLH—slides of cancer cells, which were indeed works of art.

My body did not think so. "Choose your cancer well."

I did and because of this I had my own room—ensuite—for the 11 months I was an inpatient. I had a wall, my wall, which became an art galley of images chosen by others to show their love and compassion when words were inadequate. I was sent more than 300 cards as well as poetry, music and letters during my stay in hospital. These images became points of contact with many members of staff, family and friends, conversational pieces that connected me to the outside world and normality.

What I did not know until after my stay in hospital was that a person deep in the Trust headquarters had deemed that cards etc. should not be put up on walls, as they would mark the fabric of the building. When I learnt about this, two thoughts came into my mind: firstly, that he had never had to stare at a blank wall for days on end; and secondly, that he was a very serious Zen Buddhist practitioner.

Here I must state the importance of art in hospitals. Works of art allow patients to talk with complete strangers, to make vital connections on many levels.

I watched as my cancer destroyed my body to the point where I could only breath for eight seconds without an oxygen mask; where I was being transfused blood every four hours as my body could not retain it; bore witness as my body went into full organ failure and the decision was made to stop the chemo. I came through that first skirmish with cancer. A few months later it returned.

With cancer as my companion, I relinquished my body to my amazing medical teams. I created a complex world of imagery—the world of Anaconda—where I would spend my days. A world of rivers, jungles, waterfalls, mountains, deserts and long sandy beaches where family and friends joined me. We built a village in the treetops and ate, read, played, sang, walked, swam, rode, surfed, laughed and chanted. Each day I walked to the waterfall and sat behind the diamond studded cascades of water and watched the world from within this space of healing.

Here there was no " What if …".
Here I was held safe, secure and loved unconditionally.
Here I was in the state of bliss.

Night after night, when the daily intensive chemo regime had concluded, I visualised a number of little helpers, who hoovered the grey toxins from my body into carriages under the bed. When all the carriages were full the train—red and turquoise—would trundle under the door of my room go along the corridor and, reaching the toxic medical waste cupboard, the contents would be emptied into the correct bins. The train, now yellow and sapphire, would then trundle back and the process would start again.

But the most awe inspiring and beautiful part of the whole journey was the bone marrow transplant, donated by my wonderful, selfless donor, an unknown male under the age of 40. For me this was literally my bag for life, and of life. The most exquisite shimmering rose pink, warm in tone, and of all the myriad of procedures I underwent the quickest at 20 minutes.

For each of the new bone marrow cells, I visualised a set of yellow and blue Dolce and Gabbana hats, mittens and bootees so that they would be warm. A duvet each, so that they felt safe and secure. Individual A–Zs, as this was a new country and they would need help to re-orientate themselves. Lastly, a cell phone, so that each night they could call home, and speak to their so called "father", knowing that they were loved. In the days following the transplant I would talk to each cell, reassuring them that they were fine.

On a psychotherapeutic level I was preparing myself for this life-changing event. I was deeply aware that if my body rejected the transplant, I would die.

Exhausted, to the power of a million, I would focus on a picture on my wall and allow myself to dissolve and merge with the image, to become that other, the sun, the moon and the stars; to walk in the woods, smell the grass, feel the touch of spring rain on my skin; the taste of salt on my mouth, the touch of someone's hand in mine. Then, all that would dissolve and I was just being held.

Two commentators sum up my experience:
The first the Buddha, who gave a mantra to his disciples:
"Atma Deepobhava"—become your light.

Vedic thought emphasises that the light is within you. You are not the body, you are an effulgent spirit. When the body falls apart, the spirit that resides in it goes elsewhere. The spirit is not the house. It lives in the house and looks after it. We are separate from our bodies.

The second, Joseph Campbell in *The Hero with a Thousand Faces* describes well what many others and I have experienced in profound illness.[2]

> that anyone undertakes for themselves the perilous journey into the darkness by descending either intentionally or unintentionally into the crooked lanes of her own spiritual labyrinth, she soon finds herself in a landscape of symbolical figures... and sacred mountains.... This is the second stage of the Way, that of 'purification of the self', when the senses are cleansed and humbled, and the energies and interests 'concentrated on transcendental things'.

2. Campbell, Joseph, *Collected Works of Joseph Campbell*, Novato, CA: New World Library, 2012, p. 84.

In reality these are psychological constituent parts, not real properties. People generate these images when they invest emotional time and effort into an object. It is irreplaceable AND it is sacred. That is what my experience of cancer became.

For centuries the mortal and the sacred went hand in hand. Both body and soul were tended to.

One of the best examples of this is the Hotel Die built in 1435 by Nicolas Rollin and his wife Guiyang de Sallies for the sick and infirm of Baume in southeast France. At the hotel, 12 infirm citizens lay in four-poster beds, curtained in red cloth, six on each side of the hall. At the top of the chapel was a rail dividing the mortal from the spiritual. Their bodily needs were administered to as the monks chanted for their souls.

So I leave you with two questions, from the other side; from the other side where I experienced not only world-class medical care, which is why I am standing here today, but profound other experiences beyond words.

Can art depict cancer? and
What makes a masterpiece?

Many years ago I stood before the *Beheading of John the Baptist* by Caravaggio in St John's Co-Cathedral in Valetta, Malta, the December light flooding across the side chapel, where on the back wall this painting hangs almost in darkness. After a while, as my eyes became accustomed to the light, what slowly emerged from the gloom of the canvas was a masterpiece. The painting had additional properties over and beyond its actual physical presence.

It had beauty. It had soul. But above and beyond theses two qualities, it depicted the sacred.

That is what I experienced on my journey with cancer. And this for me is how art can depict cancer.

So back to the matter in hand—*Anarchy in the Organism*. Each of us will have a different reaction to the piece depending on how you have experienced cancer.

But whatever the reaction—each is valid.

CANCER AND COMPLEXITY IN AN UNFOLDING WORLD

Simeon Nelson

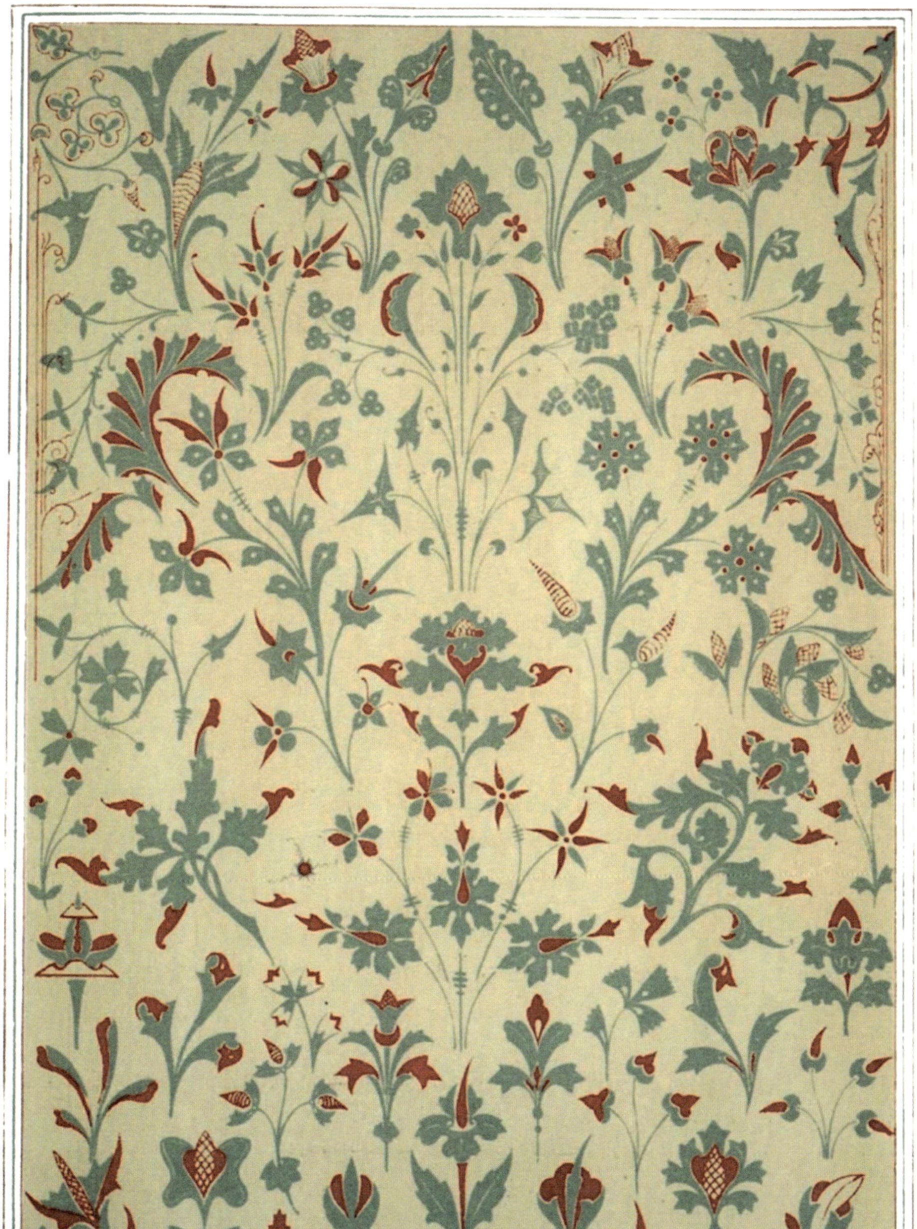

"Well-being and ill-being always contain a certain measure of their own opposite, hence they always-already in here in a hybrid relational space of liminality, an interactive territory of the middle concerned with the processes of relationship and mediation rather than with linear causality, certainty and purism."[1]

Monia Brizzi

1. Brizzi, M, "Transience and Complexity in Anarchy, Implications for Counselling Psychology", delivered at the Anarchy in the Organism symposium, Wellcome Trust, 15 July 2012.

When Guy Noble, curator at UCLH Arts, approached me to take on the subject of cancer I was excited if not a little apprehensive. I knew that this residency and commission would need to be confronted in a systematic, rigorous and personal way. I happened to be working at the time on another artwork that looked at notions of order and disorder in the cosmos and I realised that some of the same thinking could inform an approach to cancer that apprehended it both as a deeply personal, existential journey and also as a biological and social phenomenon that could be linked to other phenomena and their patterns of growth and decay, order and disorder in the natural and the social world.

Complexity theory underpins the thinking behind *Anarchy in the Organism*. Complexity theory is an integrative way of understanding whole systems and their parts that has gained wide acceptance as a way of comprehending the messy and unpredictable nature of the world in many fields such as biology and economics. I use it as an organising principle in my work and used it for this project as a way of revealing hidden underlying similarities in disparate phenomena to confront the possible meanings of cancer from scientific, social, cultural, ethical and existential perspectives.

The artwork that resulted from this residency was installed in the Capper Street windows of the Macmillan Cancer Centre. Four 55-inch video screens were mounted vertically against the glass in the window boxes facing into the street and a concentric pattern of self-adhesive vinyl on the inside surface of the glass emanated from them suggesting the connection between the system of the architecture and hospital and the artwork. The computer-generated organisms on its four video screens demonstrate growth, mutation and decay as normal aspects of being alive. With this installation I was asking whether cancer is an aberration, or an embedded aspect of being a complex organism? Complexity theory describes a reality that is non-deterministic, in which the future cannot be predicted with any degree of certainty, there is no linear causality, rather sets of probabilities and likelihoods fan out from any given moment;

PREVIOUS PAGE Branching aesthetics of ornamental systems as depicted by Owen Jones in his book, *The Grammar of Ornament*, 1858.

indeterminacy, chance and choice are intrinsic to being in the world. As Jorge Castillo-Sepúlveda and Francisco Tirado in their essay for this book put it, each moment can be seen as a recursive network of causes and consequences.

From the perspective of complexity, nature, society and humans are balanced on a razors edge between order on one side—frozen stasis where there is no freedom or agency—and chaos, on the other—a state of total disorder and flux where no definable thing can arise. This boundary between the two is where, as complexity theorist Stuart Kauffman says, novel, complex and creative phenomena occur. Complexity accounts for the generative agency of nature, the endless evolutionary experimentation that characterises life. To me, complexity also provides in some sense a rationale for empathic identification with the other, with persons, organisms, entities and things no matter how simple or complex. We are embedded in nature, inseparable

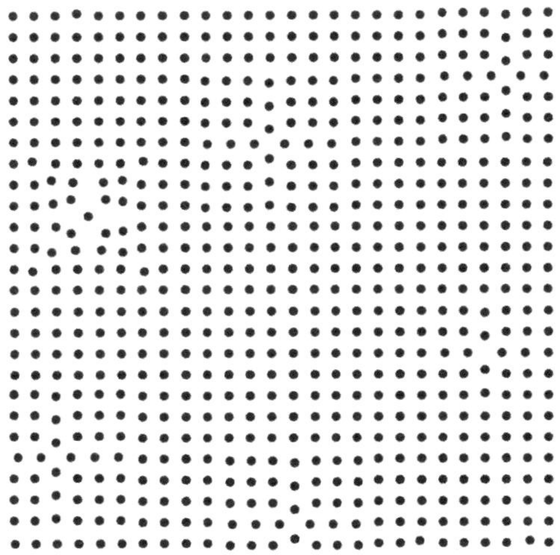

from our context; everything affects and is affected by everything else. In fact it could be said that the other is purely a linguistic category, a necessary device to be able to distinguish particular manifestations of parts of the world that are all indissolubly imbricated and intertwined. Ecologist John Muir said something similar—"When we try to pick out anything by itself we find it hitched to everything in the universe."[2]

2. Muir, John, *My First Summer in the Sierra*, 1911.

No thing is absolutely good or bad; the outcome of a process or the effect of a phenomenon is contingent on its relations with the

ABOVE *Infinitesimal*, wall drawing, 240 x 240 cm, Simeon Nelson, 2007. Depiction of the tendency toward disorder in a crystalline matrix, a precursor to the artists thinking on *Anarchy in the Organism.*

other processes and phenomena it affects and is affected by. I see similarities in this metaphysic to Bruno Latour's actor-network theory in which there are no indivisible substances or essences on one hand or, on the other, nothing resembling the self-referential language games invoked by relativists as the only possible constituent of reality.[3] His thinking points beyond the primacy of the subject, the percipient ego to an understanding that sees the object in some ways as prior to and creative of the subject.

3. Latour, Bruno et al., *Reassembling the Social: An Introduction to Actor-Network-Theory*, Oxford: Oxford University Press, 2007.

Complexity theory provides an integrative way of looking at apparently disparate phenomena, from the stock market to social change, from cancer to population dynamics and epidemiology. By generating the artwork through the visual patterns of complexity, I was trying to draw out analogies between cancer and many different types of social and cultural systems. I see structural and meaningful relationships between the growth patterns and social interactions of, to name a few examples, cities, vegetation cover, populations, and cancer. It was a primary aim of the artwork to draw out comparisons between these patterns and thereby render cancer as a more knowable and situated phenomenon to a broad audience.

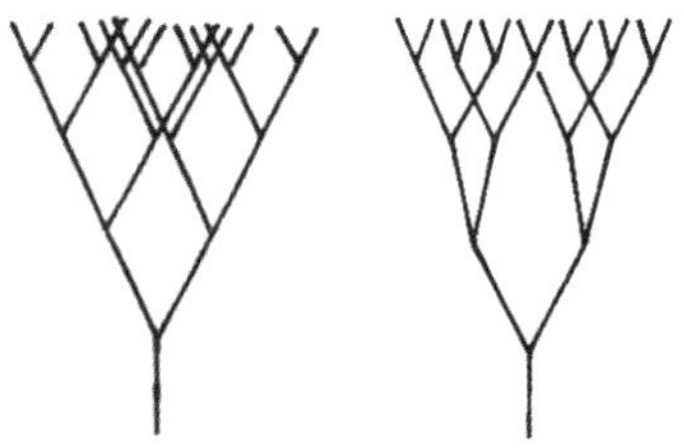

Complexity theory sees an inherent creativity in nature—an endless innovation as a fundamental given. This is an idea that replaces deterministic, reductionist and linear 'laws' of nature with an organic, evolving creative imperative unfolding ceaselessly at the base of reality. Complexity and emergence imply a process rather than a substance ontology and imbue nature, as Stuart Kauffman noted in his recent book, *Reinventing the Sacred*, with an inherent sacredness.[4] This reverence or sense of innate worth and preciousness constitutes a beauty that allows a deep identification, a dissolution of object and subject, observer and observed. It is a vision of reality that demands a creative apprehension; it demands an ethics of creative participation because we are part of the world and the world is part of us.

4. Kaufman, Stuart A, *Reinventing the Sacred: A New View of Science, Reason, and Religion*, New York: Basic Books, 2008.

I began to see cancer as a form of processual interplay between actors, between itself and the body it is embedded in. These actors constitute a network of relations, rather than a collection of isolated concrete "things"; any form of growth arises out of a flux of vital internal and external purposes—they are telic, they strive toward their own ends. By situating cancer within a wider context of complex evolving systems from cities to trees to landscapes, *Anarchy in the Organism*

ABOVE Lindenmayer Systems generated from simple algebra. Branching organisations are intrinsic to ornamental, computational and natural systems.

attempts a reconciliation of cancer as a normative part of being in the world. Life is a process that ends in death, and it is this finitude that imbues life with meaning and beauty. Monia Brizzi had a major influence on my thinking by bringing her perspective as a counselling existential psychologist to bear on the problem I was trying to apprehend. Her vision of life as a process of flourishing and perishing, of our creaturely situatedness in a dynamical world, extended my thinking on complexity to the fundamental fact of the contingency of our embedded existence. We discussed the interplay between mind, body and the world. Suffering and joy are intrinsic to being alive. Death is in the process of living; we are all dying, organically and experientially as we live. *Anarchy in the Organism* (*AitO*) perhaps also perhaps touches on fear of death, and a reticence around death in modern British society. Death has been marginalised, removed from our experience by a medical industry that sees illness or ill-being as a scientific problem and sequesters more and more of the process of dying to hospital wards. As Monia points out in her essay for this book, our positivist humanist society exhorts us to flourish and prosper, to relegate death and serious illness to the unspeakable shadows. *AitO* represents the morbidity amidst vitality. It can be read as a *memento mori* as in Poussin's painting, *Et in Arcadia Ego*, of ancient Greek shepherds contemplating a tomb in an idyllic landscape, a warning that death stalks the most flourishing and delightful moments of life and we forget that at our peril.

This situated understanding of cancer as an intrinsic aspect of being, of being an organism to *me*, can make, what happens—even terrible things that are largely outside a persons control—more comprehensible, more bearable, less random and appalling. Affliction and suffering are not to be avoided at all costs but accepted and integrated into one's authentic experience of being alive; *amor fati* or loving ones fate, as Nietzsche put it, becomes a source of resilience, equanimity and hope. I am awed with the biology of the body and the becomingness of the human person. How does an organism assemble itself and how do people maintain a sense of self within the growing and aging process?

For many years I have worked with the visualisation of science. I have used icons such as the (misleading) Bohr atom, the double helix of the DNA molecule and Ernst Haeckel's[5] seminal and influential image of the Darwinian Tree of Life in my work, so when I was contacted by UCLH I foresaw that the visualisation, the making comprehensible through visual representation would be central to my approach. How we perceive and understand science and medicine is contingent on

5. Ernst Heinrich Philipp August Haeckel (16 February 1834–9 August 1919) was an important German biologist, naturalist, philosopher, physician, professor and artist who discovered, described and named thousands of new species, mapped a genealogical tree relating all life forms, and coined many terms in biology, including anthropogeny, ecology, phylum, phylogeny, stem cell, and the kingdom. He was a leading proponent of Darwinism.

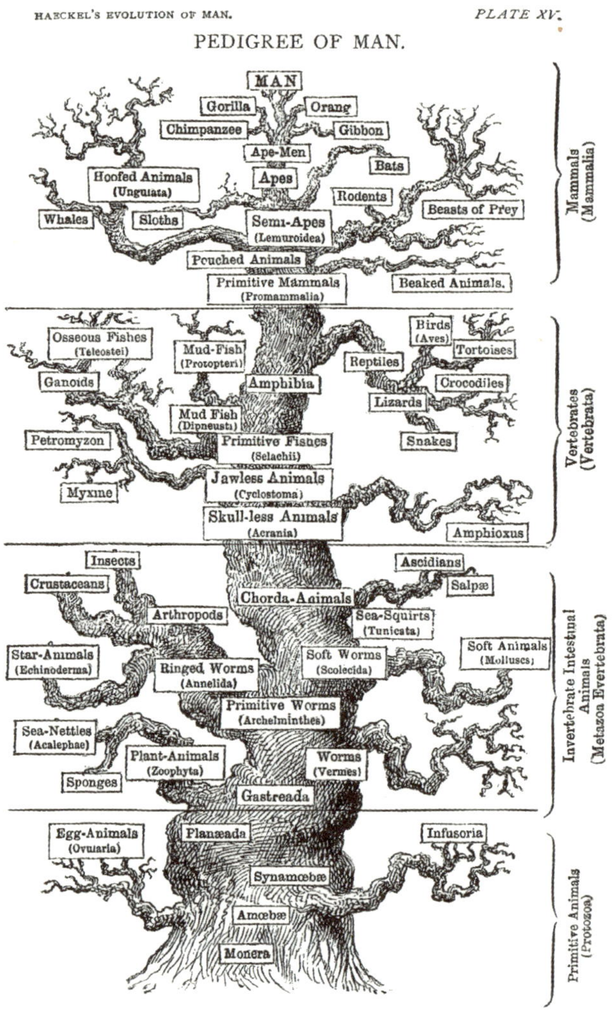

how we consume the representations of them; even scientists claim that they cannot 'know' something in their field without being able to visualise it, without having an iconic image to flesh out the data.

I use representations of patterns as much as the patterns themselves, from the sciences and ethnographic/architectural ornament. I elide computational and ornamental representations of organic form. For example, the tree-geometry that is the basis of the *AitO* organisms

ABOVE The Tree of Life as depicted by Ernst Haeckel in the *The Evolution of Man*, 1879.

is an L-system algorithm that can be used to digitally replicate real trees with remarkable accuracy. Tree-forms are found in different ornamental systems from around the world and my collaborators and I used these to map the blood vessel networks of organs in the body. The technique of isolating an element, extracting its topological[6] essence and removing it from its context allows the combining of fragments from different formal, aesthetic and real systems and is part of an ongoing practice of what I call 'relational or recombinant taxonomy'. This search for underlying similarities not immediately apparent is motivated by an intuition that under the diversity and complexity of things there are sets of relationships that, if followed far enough, ultimately connect to the same source.

6. Topology is the study of the innate properties of form that remain invariant under distortion.

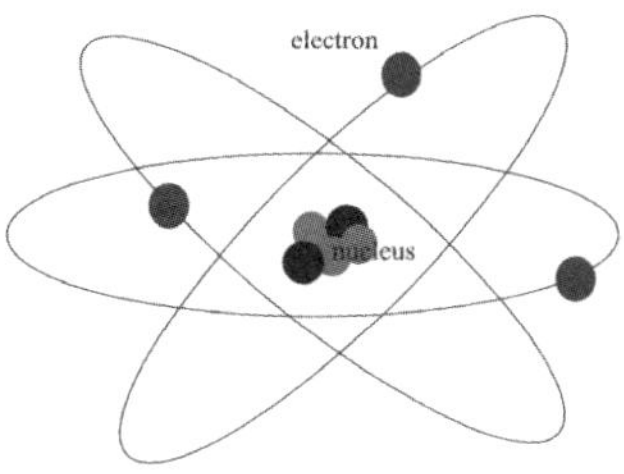

AitO visualises cancer as a complex adaptive system arising within the body that is in turn embedded in a social system of consumption and lifestyle factors. Cancer is by its nature non-local; after metastasis it cannot be cut out, cannot be separated from the body it is afflicting.

My interviews and consultations with patients, their carers and clinicians had a huge impact on the creative process. There were strong negative initial reactions from a patient care representative and an artist who was working as a facilitator with cancer patients. They found my preliminary work and thinking graphic and disturbing in the sense that I had tried to depict cancer as a malignant growth invading the tissues of the organism analogically, by conflating this phenomenon with urban growth in a series of drawings.

The patient response posed an important question about the role of art in the context of a cancer hospital. *AitO* unapologetically tries to confront the suffering caused by cancer. I was pleased on one level that the reaction had been strong (all artists appreciate such reactions!) but I realised that I could not operate purely autonomously with a constituency that needed to be cared for. This points to the open-ended and ongoing debate around artistic autonomy and instrumentalism—art in the service of some extrinsic aim or benefit, or art for art's sake. Thankfully my work did not elicit such strong reactions from other patients I interviewed in my studio. It was demanding and affecting to interview them, their representatives and their carers.

I maintain a hope that this approach could lead to a more holistic understanding of cancer, and may even in a way have a role in

ABOVE Model of the Bohr Atom, a very influential (and misleading) visualising of the atom.

developing new approaches to understanding patient perspectives and also the patient's—or their loved ones'—understanding of what is happening to them. I wanted to bring the science of cancer into contact with the patient's experience of it on a broader canvas.

The challenge has been to work with cancer as both a fascinating organic phenomenon with underlying structural similarities to other growth processes and also as a life or death encounter for sufferers. *AitO* evolved to encompass both these perspectives and the contribution to the public understanding of cancer as a complex

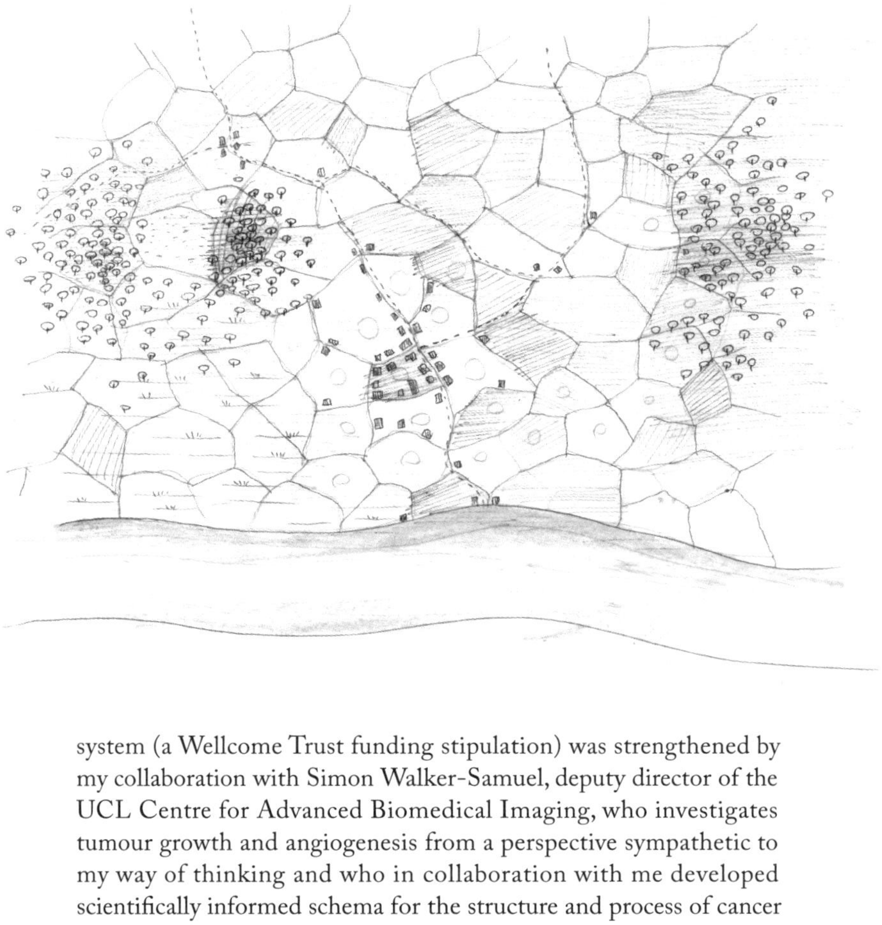

system (a Wellcome Trust funding stipulation) was strengthened by my collaboration with Simon Walker-Samuel, deputy director of the UCL Centre for Advanced Biomedical Imaging, who investigates tumour growth and angiogenesis from a perspective sympathetic to my way of thinking and who in collaboration with me developed scientifically informed schema for the structure and process of cancer development that occurs in the installation. With Simon and Nick Rothwell I generated real-time iterative cancer topologies that grew like tumours within abstracted venous networks.

PP 32–35 *Oncoburg* series, pen on A3 paper, Simeon Nelson, 2011. Cartographic drawings based on textbook diagrams of a tumour growing into surrounding tissue causing angiogenesis, the growing of its own blood vessel network.

ABOVE *Oncogenetic 1*, pen on A3 paper, Simeon Nelson, 2011.

My first experiments with depicting cancer as a complex system tried to capture the process of tumour growth. I made a sequence of drawings based on illustrations of this and the way tumours co-opt the body's blood supply, generating new veins to supply their exponential growth. They made an explicit analogy between tumour growth and the growth of a town into the surrounding countryside. I also worked on drawings that showed the healing effect of therapies on cancer, which depict the city being reabsorbed into the natural world.

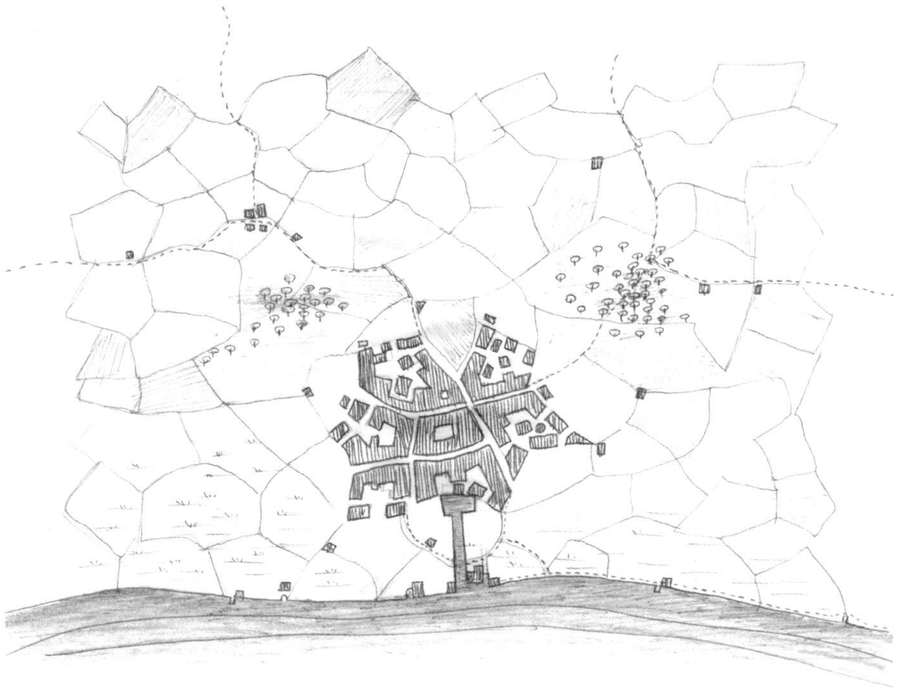

The mathematical organisms on the four screens of the installation develop cancer to varying degrees. Coded within the parameters of complexity, their survival rate is similar to that of the general population. The organisms are ambiguous and scalar; they could be the streetscapes of evolving cities disrupted by the successive impositions of changing social imaginaries, or they could be trees, for example. The tumours growing chaotically within the organisms have detached themselves from the autopoiesis of the body and have become a breakaway entity competing with the body for resources.[7]

ABOVE *Oncogenetic 2*, pen on A3 paper, Simeon Nelson, 2011.

7. Autopoiesis: (from Greek αὐτο- (auto-), meaning "self", and ποίησις (poiesis), meaning "creation, production") literally "self-creation". The term was introduced in 1972 by Chilean biologists Humberto Maturana and Francisco Varela.

The cartographic aesthetic I used for the preliminary drawings was drawn from maps of London's suburban growth before the age of mass transit in the nineteenth century. This aesthetic system was abandoned for a more directly scientifically informed depiction of the process of angiogenesis co-developed by myself, Simon Walker-Samuel and Nick Rothwell, the artist and software developer who brought his interest in mathematical systems to bear by introducing Voronoi geometry as the matrix for our organisms.[8] Working with Simon illuminated my understanding of some of the mechanisms of

8. In mathematics, a Voronoi diagram is a way of dividing space into a number of regions. A set of points (called seeds, sites, or generators) is specified beforehand and for each seed there will be a corresponding region consisting of all points closer to that seed than to any other. The regions are called Voronoi cells.

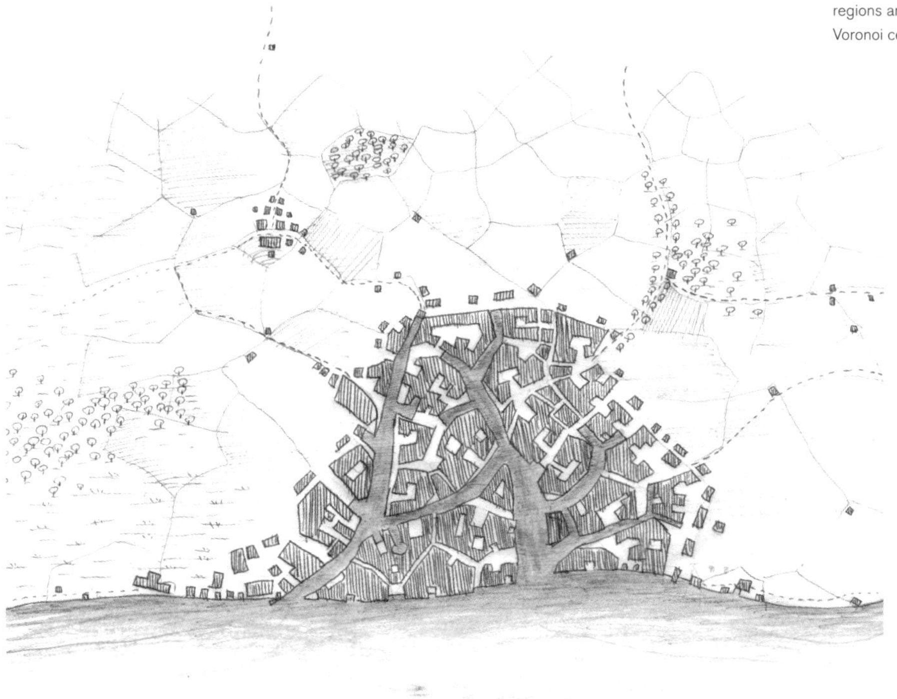

tumour growth and angiogenesis, and ensured that the organisms we co-created had a rigour, were founded in science, not simply chimeras of artistic imagination. Simon, as he points out in his essay, found working on this liberating in terms of perspective, and brought back to life wider preoccupations and conception that can be lost in the exigencies of highly focused research.

AitO is an audio-visual artwork; the music for it was composed and performed by Rob Godman, who writes on the process in his contribution to this book. It was scored to the same parameters as

ABOVE *Oncogenetic 3*, pen on A3 paper, Simeon Nelson, 2011.

the growing organisms on the screens and haunted the streetscape of the installation.

In Voltaire's satirical novella *Candide*, Dr Pangloss parodies Gottfried Leibniz's notion that the world we live in is the best one possible in the face of the absurdity, atrocity and calamity of eighteenth century Europe. In both *AitO* and *Plenum*, the other project I was working on at this time, I venture that Leibniz was correct; that despite the suffering and affliction visited on a daily basis we do in fact live in, and can only live in, 'the best of all possible worlds'.

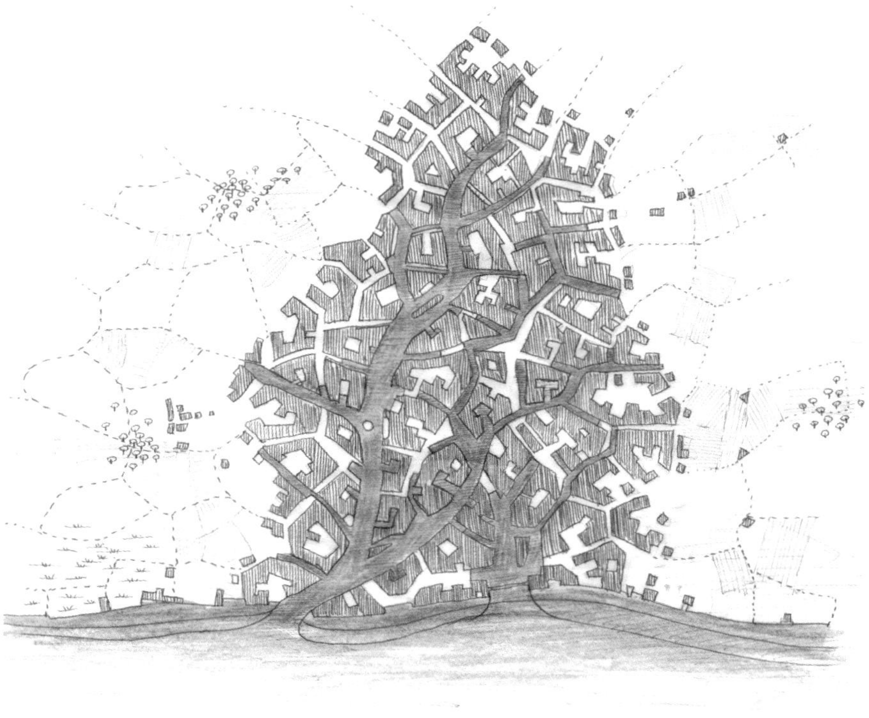

Plenum was a computer-generated, real-time architectural light projection looking at the balance of order and disorder in the cosmos. Both it and *AitO* encode the idea of a world of transience, of emergent fleeting pattern. Cancer is an unstable pattern in the body. Entropy is the irreversibility of time's arrow, the increasing randomness or disorder in a system. Our bodies are only patterns that happen to be stable enough for our lifespan and of course this stability is precarious; cancer and other disruptions can cause catastrophe. The earth is a dynamical system where plate tectonics caused by convection currents welling up from the earth's core cause continental drift, mountain ranges, volcanoes and earthquakes.

ABOVE *Oncogenetic 4*, pen on A3 paper, Simeon Nelson, 2011.

I am situating affliction and catastrophe within a 'theodicy of complexity'. Theodicy is a theological term for explanation of suffering in the world compatible with the notion of a loving God. These two works attempted to explain disease and calamity as functions of dynamic systems, necessary if complex beings like us are to evolve. Cellular mutation, ecological dynamism and evolution are part of this 'best of all possible worlds'. Cancer on a human level and tectonic rupture, earthquakes and tsunamis on a planetary level are intrinsic to this. The appearance of tumours in the organic networks of *Anarchy in the Organism* resonate with the appearance

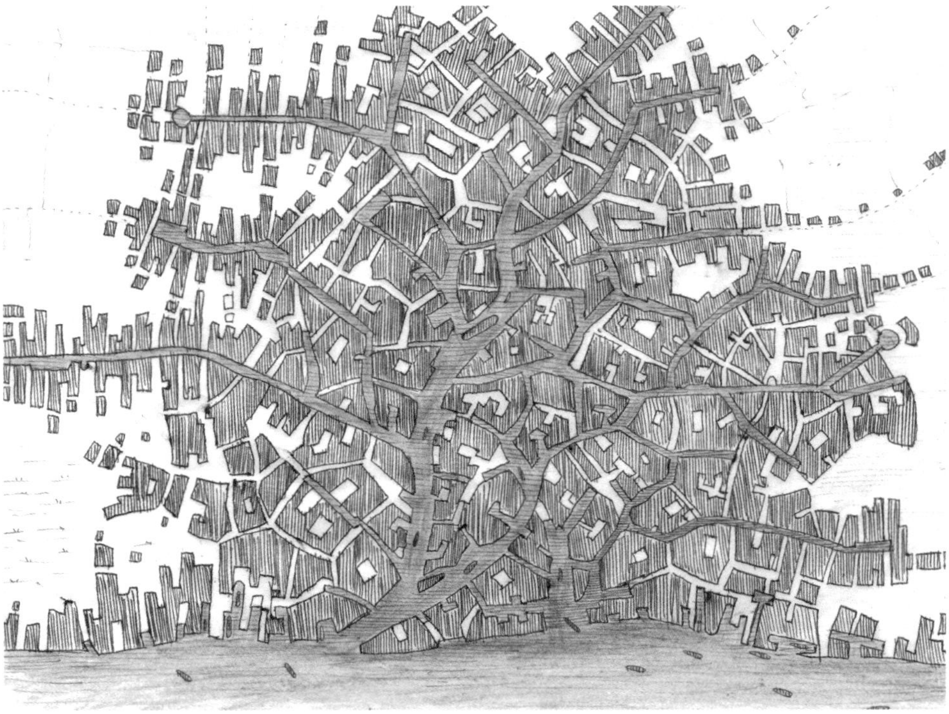

of evil in the Christian creation myth, the music of Lucifer detaching and becoming discordant with the music of creation. Both works play out as creation myths, a meditation on our creaturely, situated and contingent freedom; ultimately the relationship between created world and creator.

ABOVE *Oncogenetic 5*, pen on A3 paper, Simeon Nelson, 2011.

OPPOSITE View of a window of the Capper Street installation. Photography Sonke Faltien.

OVERLEAF Schematic drawing of the window installation, showing the monitor embedded in a self adhesive vinyl pattern and the transducer speaker positions to either side of the monitor.

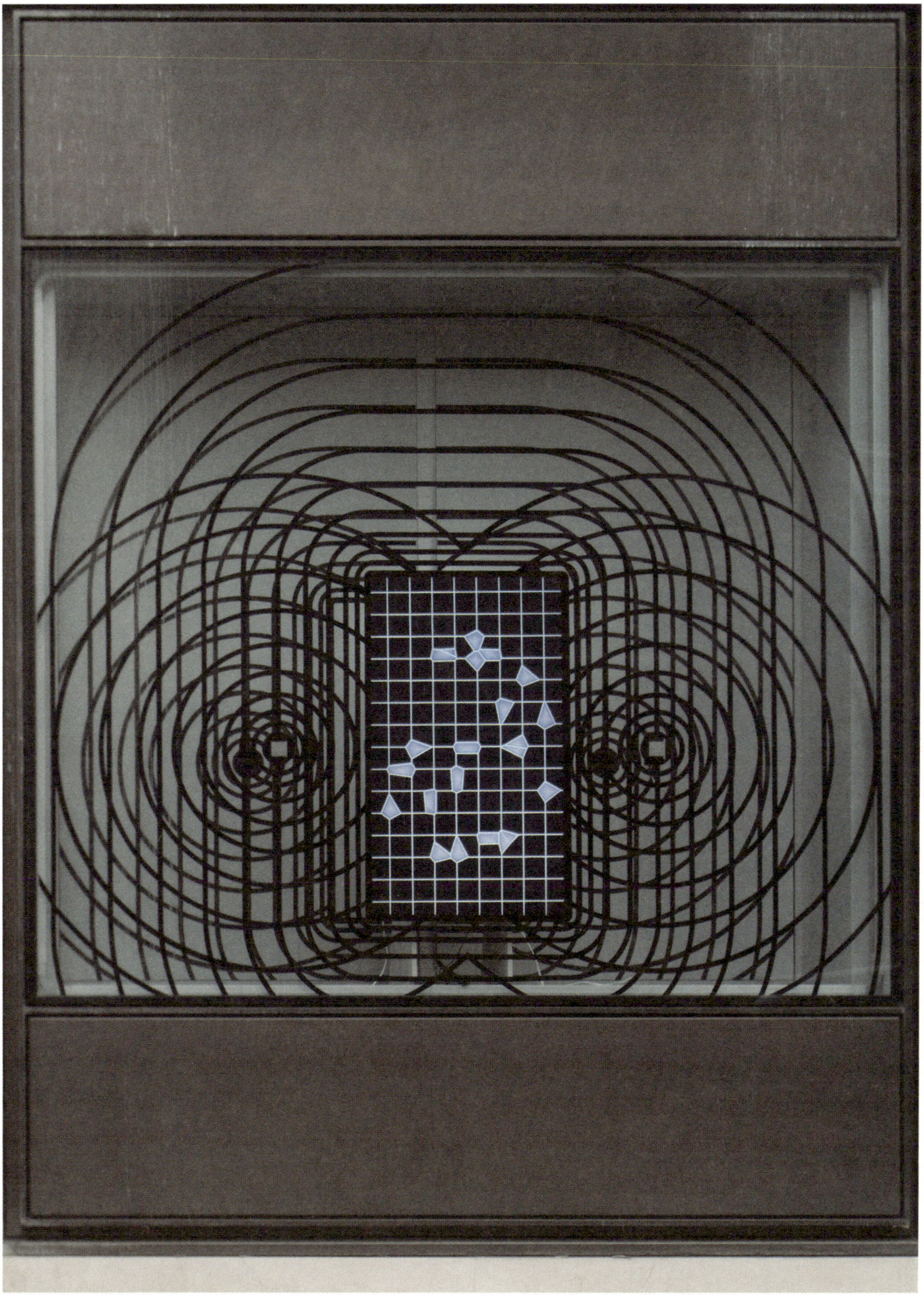

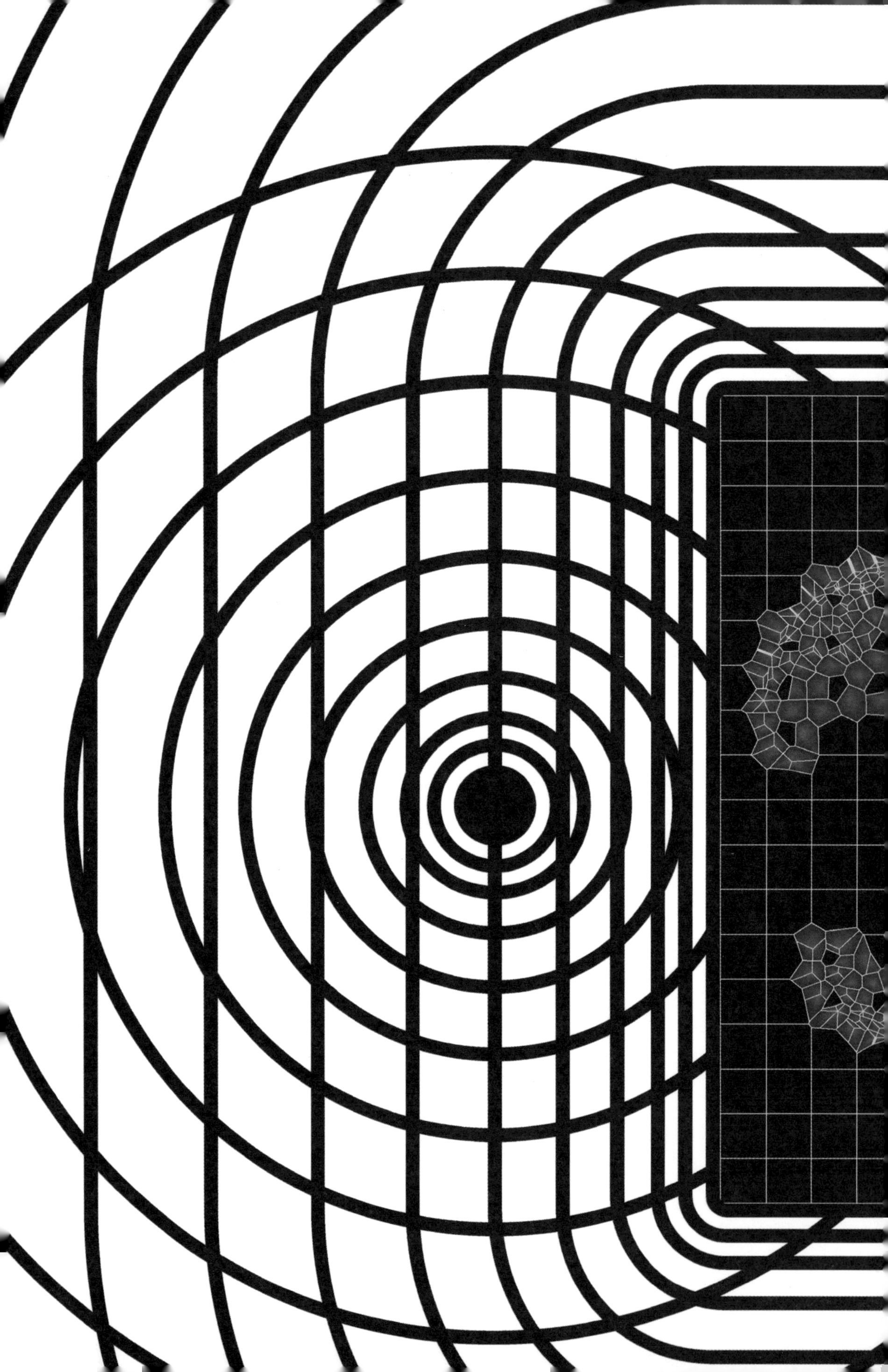

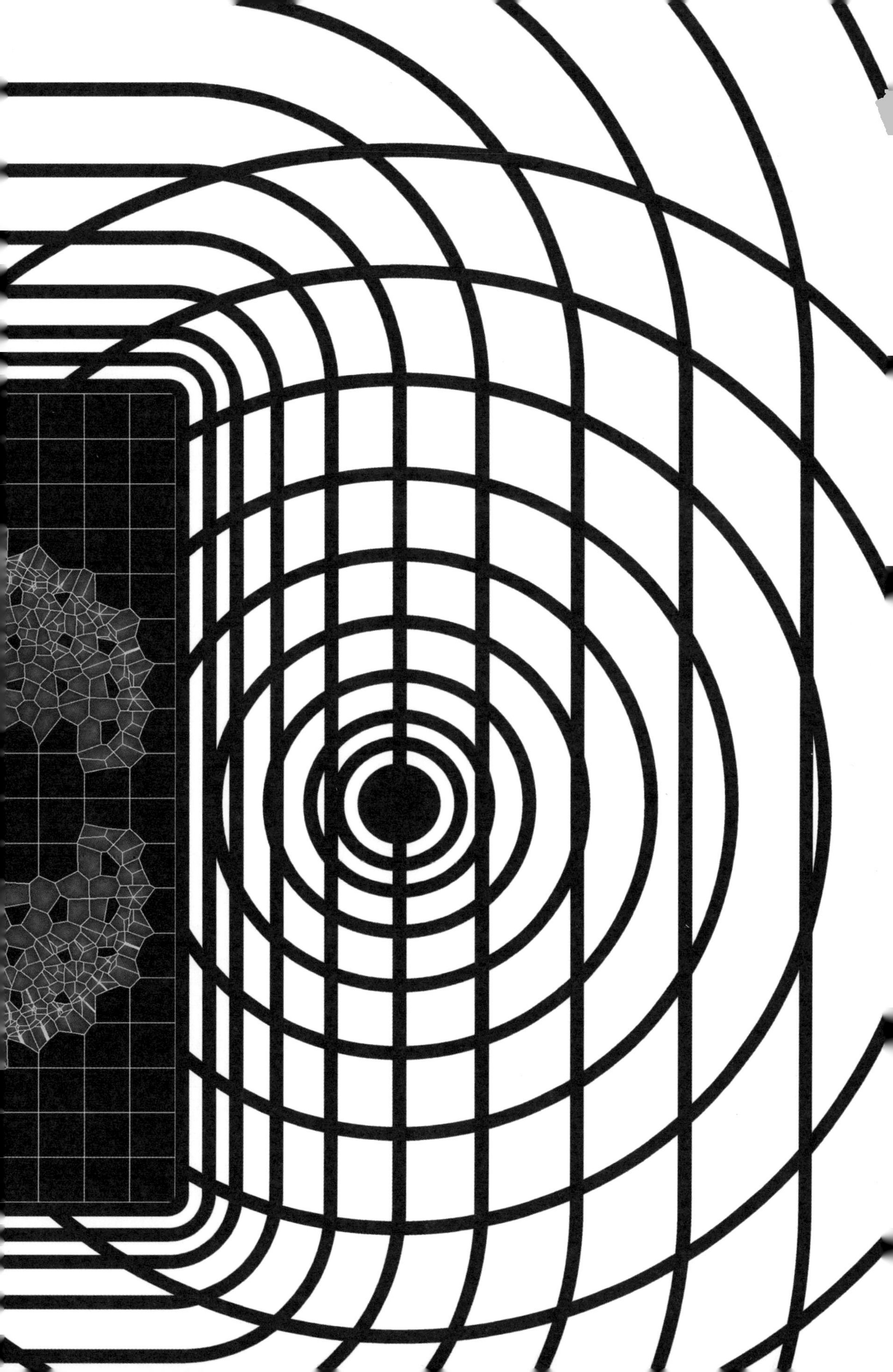

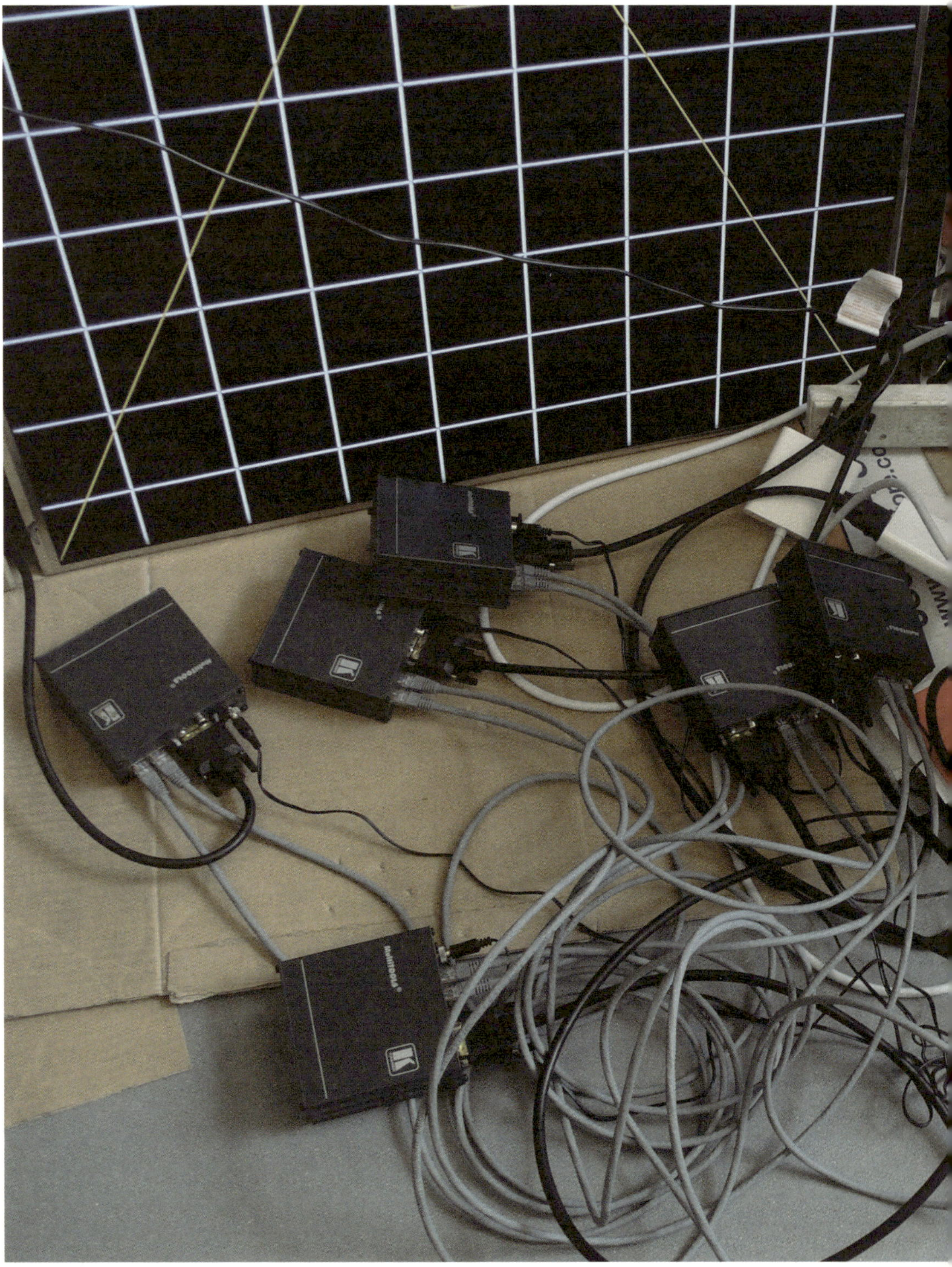

ABOVE Testing the network and the audio visual system on site. Simeon Nelson, 7 September, 13:00. Photography Nick Rothwell.

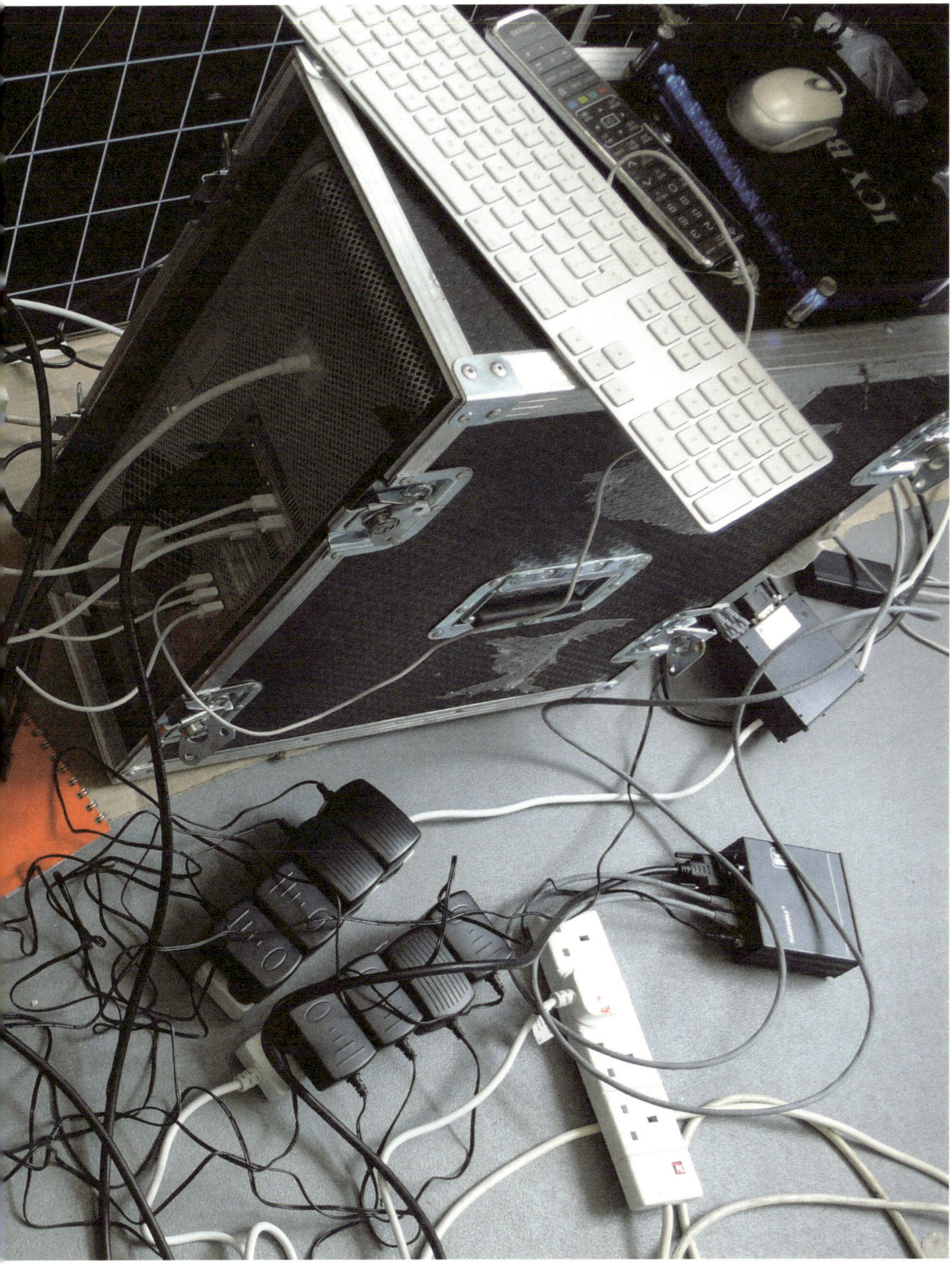
ICY BOX

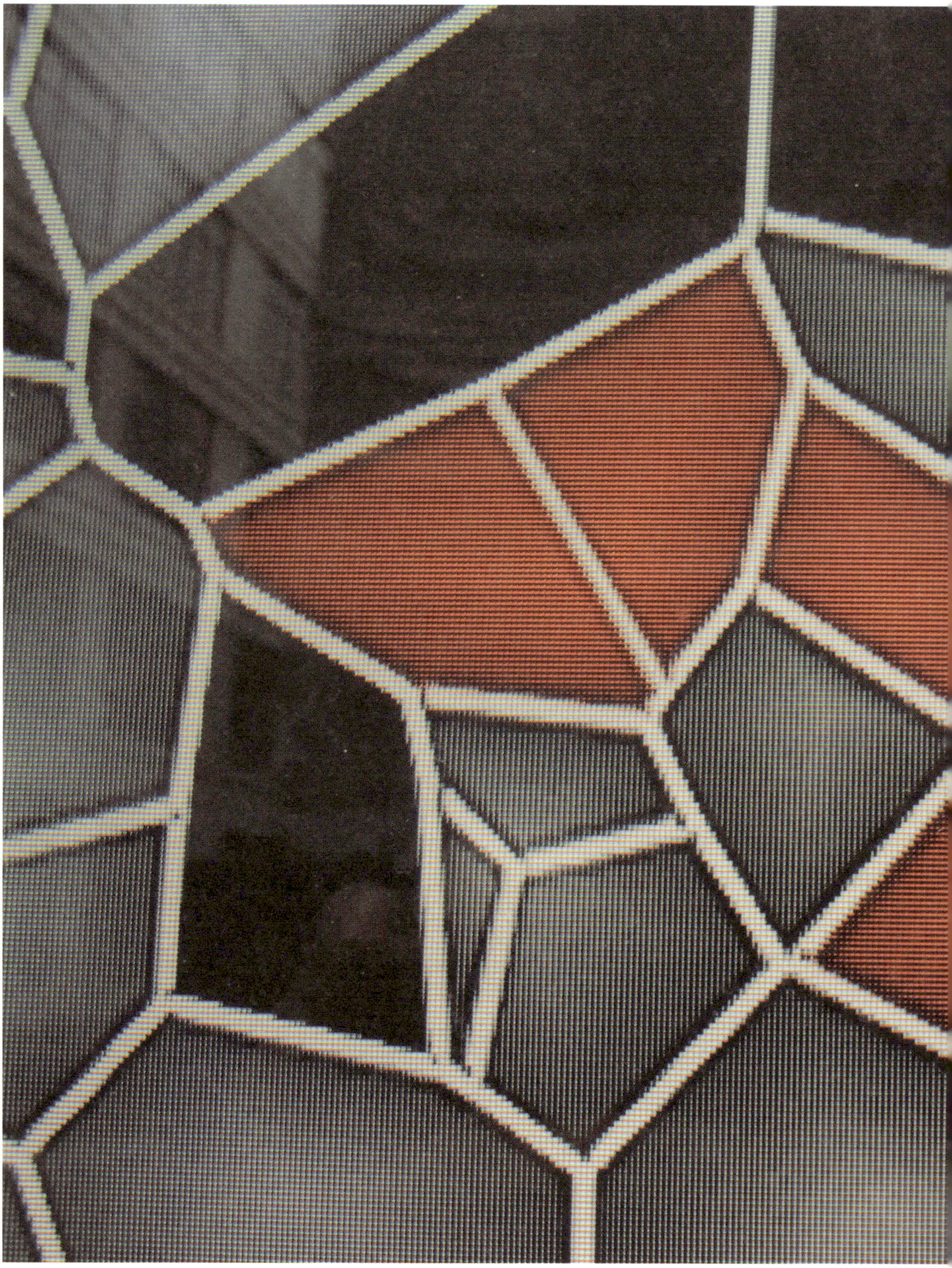

ABOVE Close up of the monitor screen showing cancerous cells growing in non-cancerous tissue. Photography Simeon Nelson.

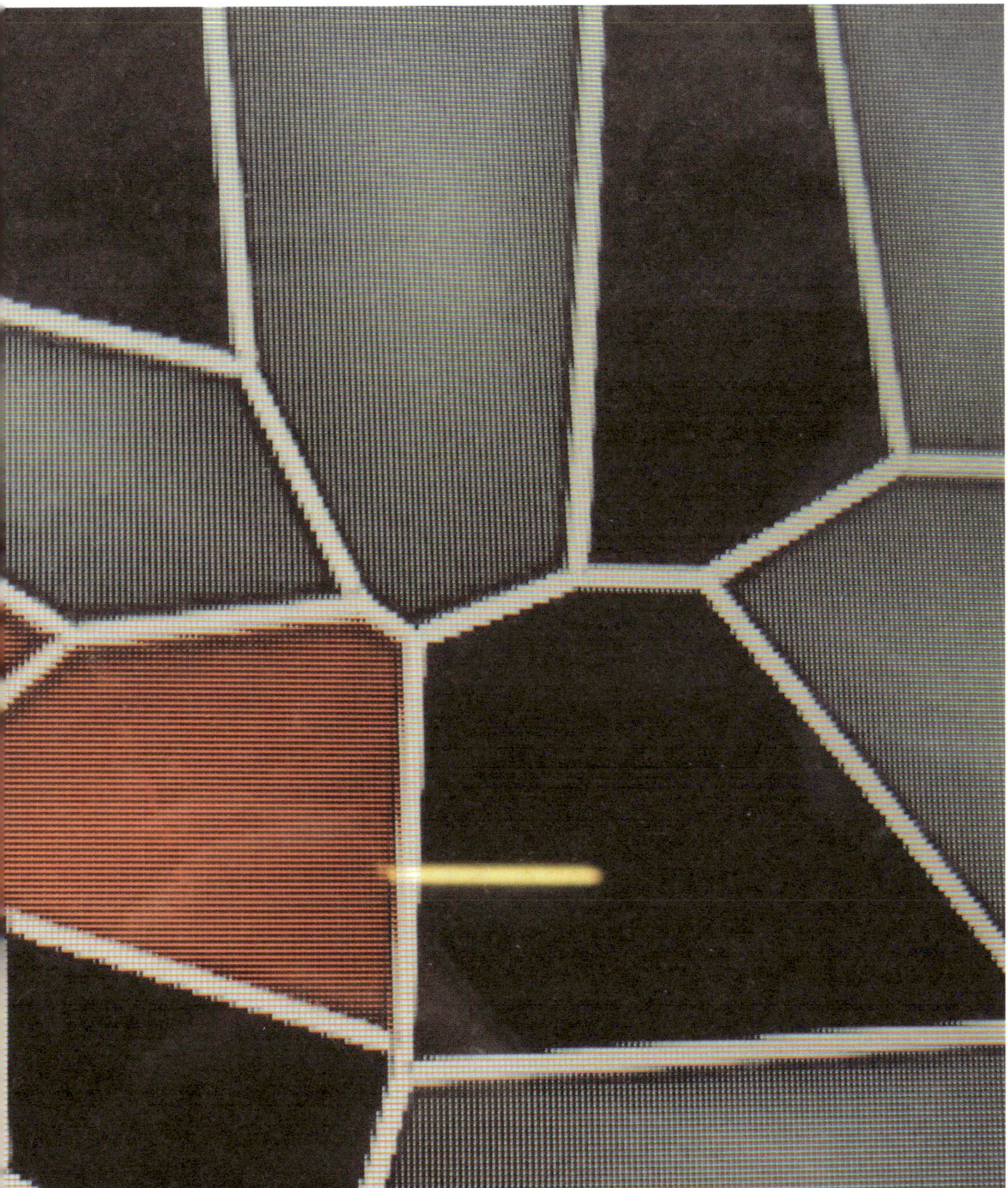

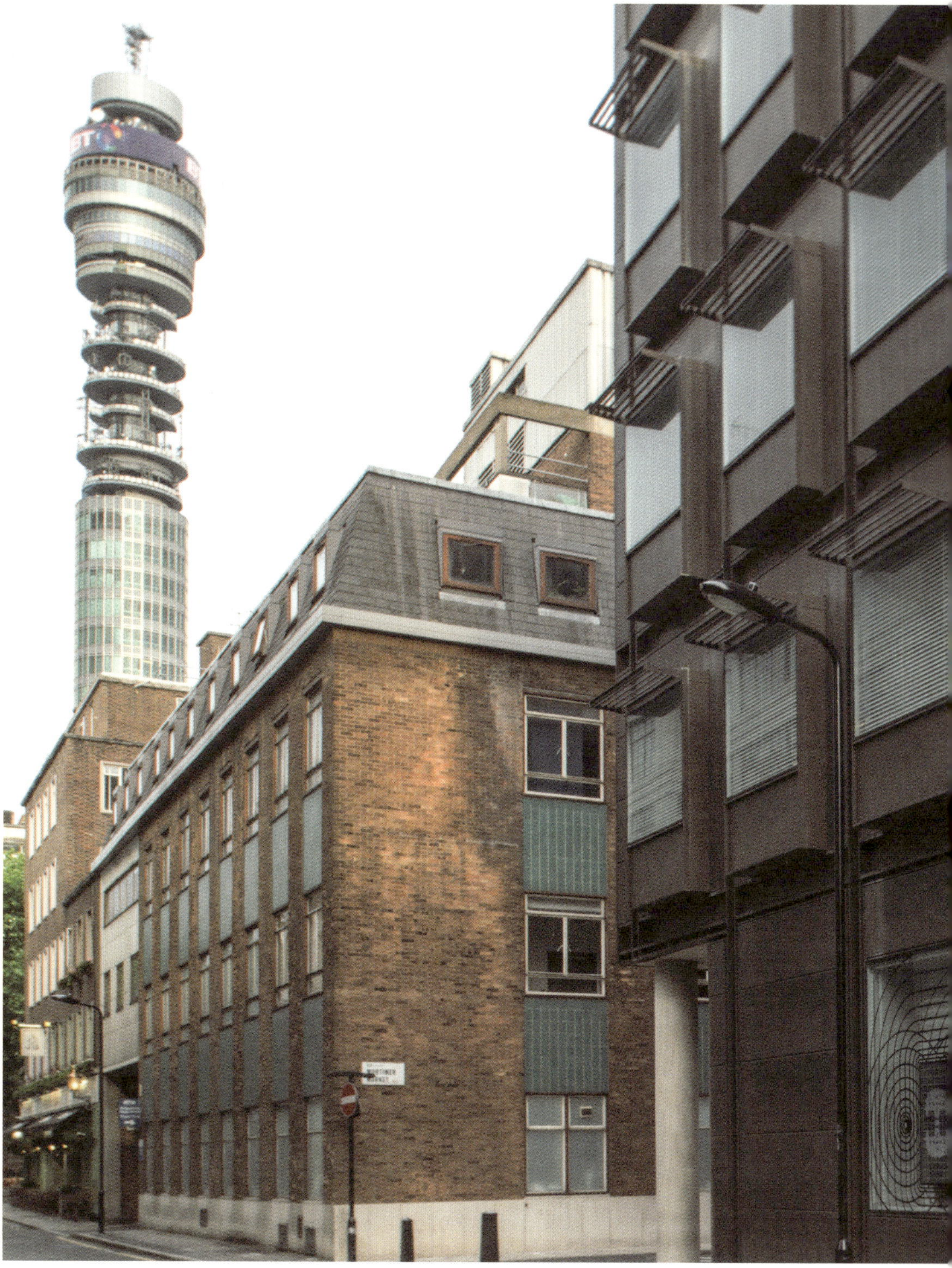

ABOVE Contextual installation view in Capper Street. Photography Sonke Faltien.

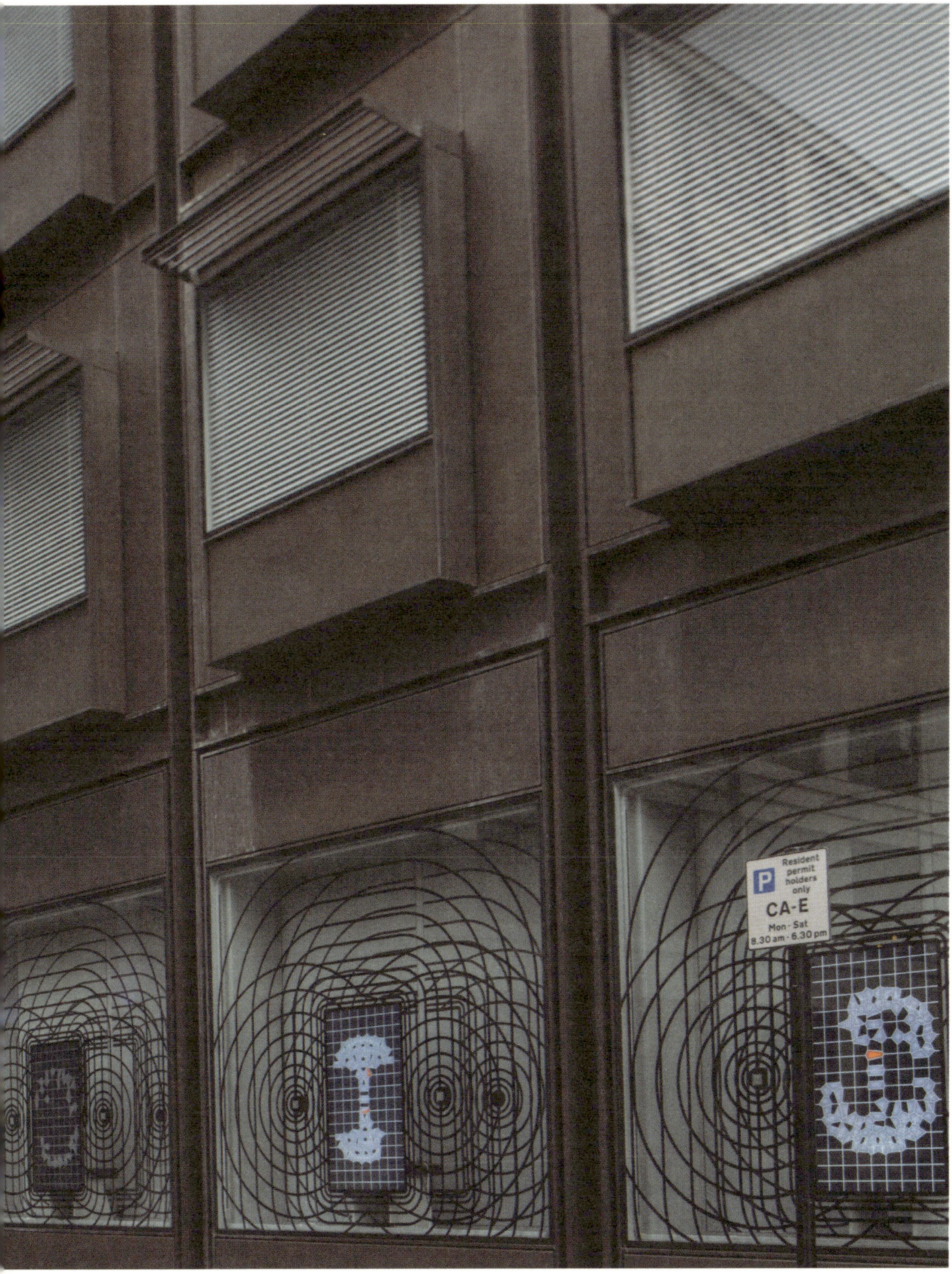
P
Resident
permit
holders
only
CA-E
Mon - Sat
8.30 am - 6.30 pm

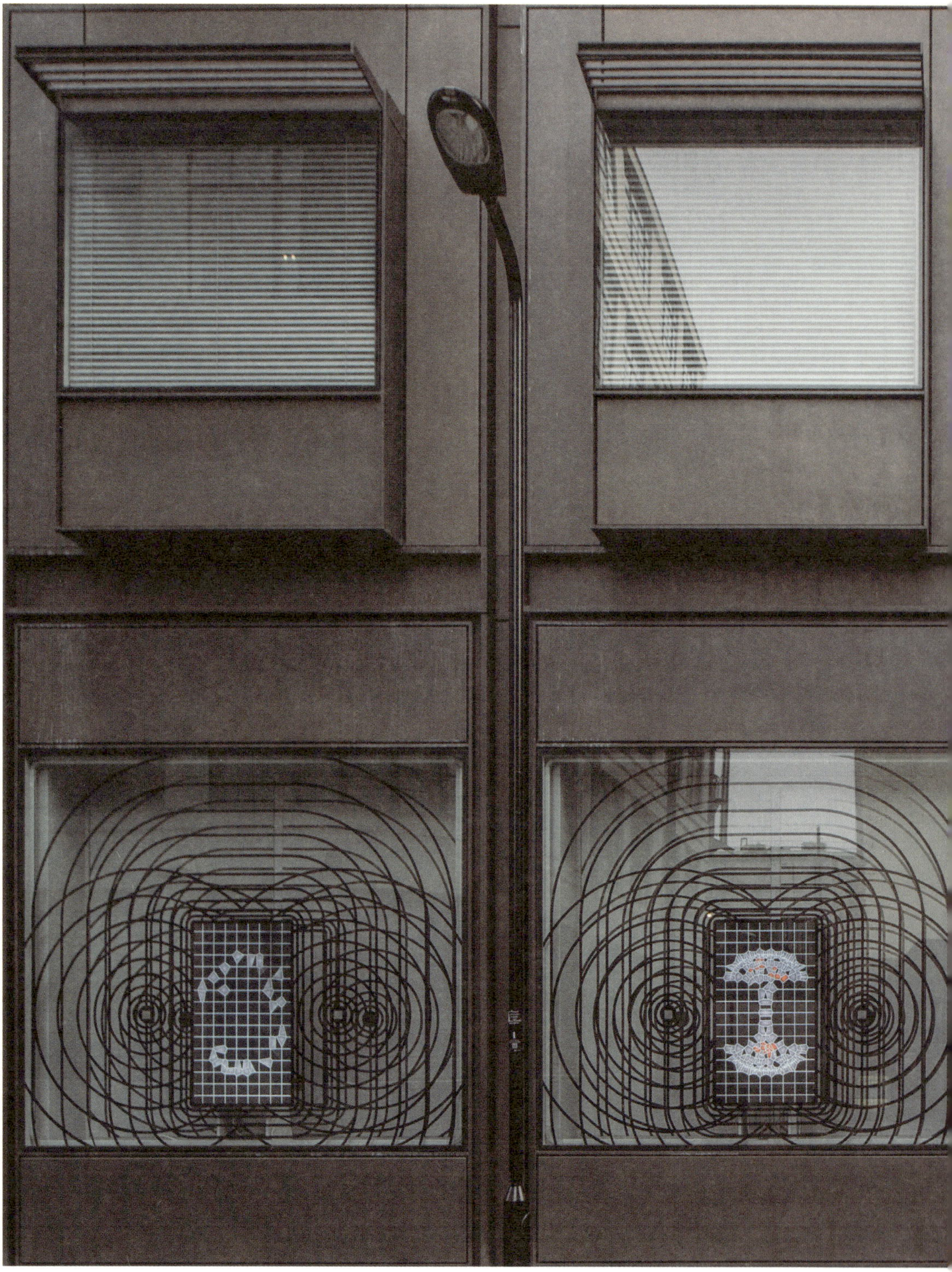

ABOVE Installation view in Capper Street.
Photography Sonke Faltien.

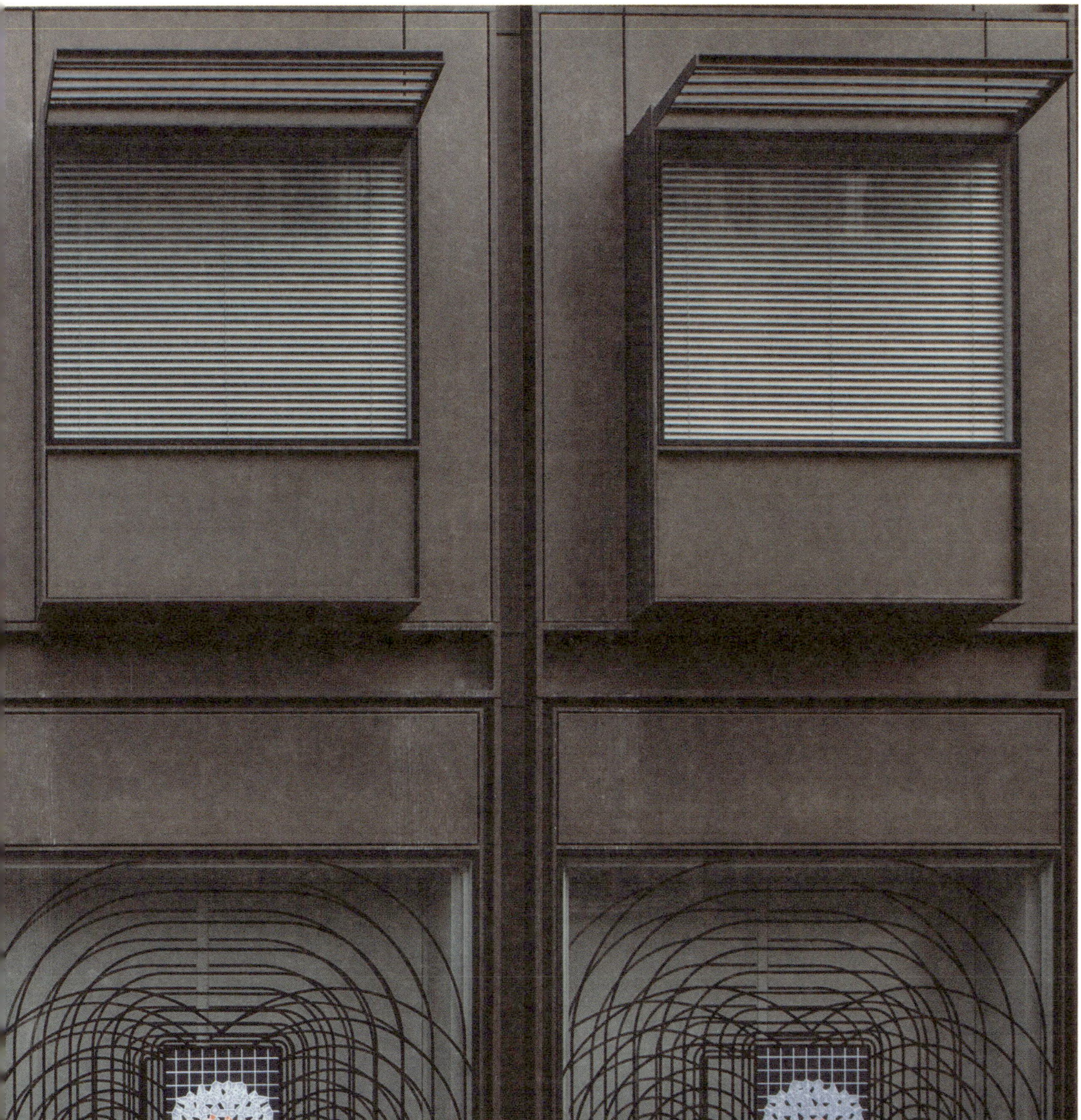

THE ARCHITECTURE OF TUMOUR BLOOD VESSEL NETWORKS

Simon Walker-Samuel

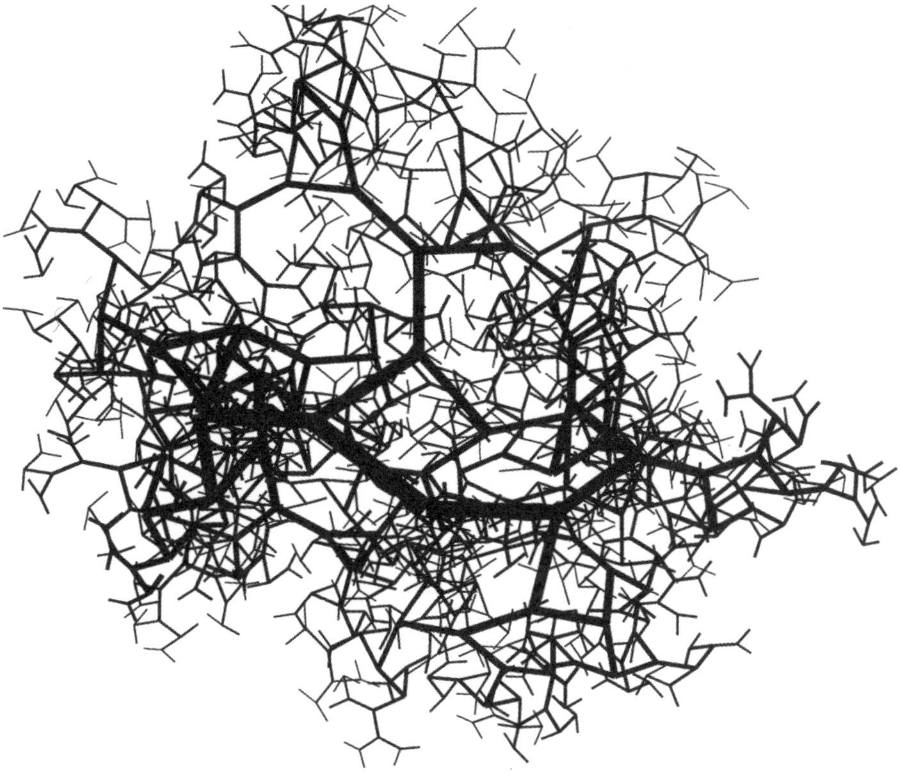

ABOVE Computer simulation of a tumour blood vessel network, Simon Walker-Samuel.

My involvement as scientific advisor on *Anarchy in the Organism* (*AitO*) began with a visit by the artist Simeon Nelson to the Centre for Advanced Biomedical Imaging (CABI), where I work as a research scientist. My research focuses on developing new methods to assess cancer physiology, non-invasively (i.e., without having to take a biopsy or make any incisions), using medical imaging devices such as magnetic resonance imaging (MRI) and x-ray computed tomography (CT). Simeon's vision for the project was based around how normal tissues can transform into a diseased, cancerous state, and to draw analogies with processes such as towns and cities becoming industrialised, and of the notion of a progression from simplicity and order, to complexity and chaos. Such analogies work well within the context of tumour growth, in which the cooperation usually evident between cells in healthy organs is replaced by rampant, unconstrained proliferation

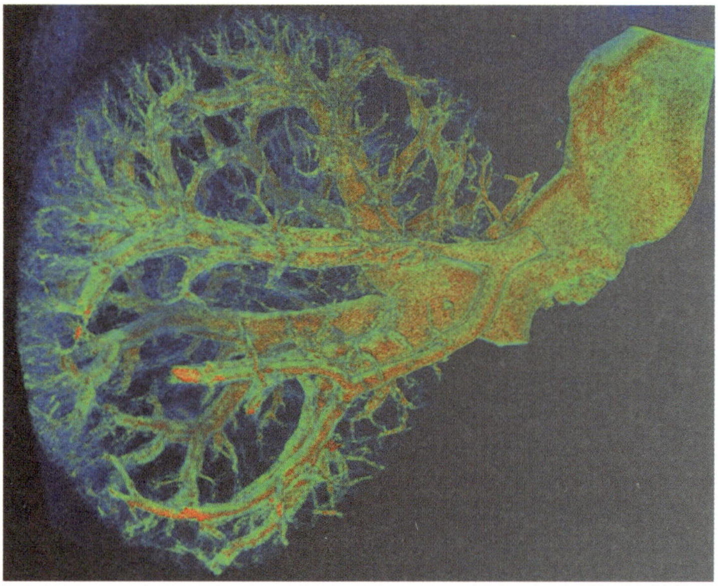

by individual cells fighting for their own, individual survival. The differences in the structure of normal tissues and that of cancerous tumours is an area that I have a long-held interest in, and so provided a shared basis for the themes and ideas that were eventually incorporated into *AitO*.

Normally, the replication of cells in the human body is constrained by a combination of genetics and interactions with the surrounding environment. In tumours, mutations in the genetic code cause these control mechanisms to become deregulated, and results in rapid,

ABOVE Blood vessel network in a mouse kidney, revealed using x-ray computed tomography, Jake Burrell.

unconstrained replication. By reproducing in such an uncontrolled manner the cells initially form a small, densely packed cluster, whose demands outstrip the supply of nutrients available (in particular, oxygen). In an attempt to improve their situation, the cells send out chemical distress signals that are detected by nearby blood vessels, and which respond by forming new branches towards the tumour.[1] The process by which a dedicated blood supply is developed is known as angiogenesis, and is a key element of tumour growth; without blood vessels, growth cannot continue.[2] However, the intensity of the chemical distress signals sent by the tumour is such that the resulting network of blood vessels is rapidly formed, but is poorly and inefficiently constructed.[3]

1. Folkman, J, "Role of angiogenesis in tumor growth and metastasis", *Semin Oncol*, 29 (6 Suppl 16), 2002, pp. 15–18.

2. Hanahan, D and RA Weinberg, "The hallmarks of cancer", *Cell*, 100, 1, 2000, pp. 57–70.

3. Baish, JW et al., "Role of tumor vascular architecture in nutrient and drug delivery: an invasion percolation-based network model", *Microvasc Res*, 51, 3, 1996, pp. 327–346.

The structure of normal blood vessel networks has evolved in such a manner that the flow of blood is highly efficient and well organised. The body's largest artery, the aorta, projects from the top of the heart and soon branches into smaller arteries that carry blood to all regions of the body. In turn, these divide into smaller vessels called arterioles, all according to a well-defined and efficient branching pattern. At a certain size, arterioles turn into capillaries, which are structured in such a way that they allow nutrients to move from blood into the tissue. Capillaries then connect to the venous system, which funnels blood back to the heart. Both arteries and veins have a well-formed vessel wall that is surrounded by a sheet of smooth muscle that allows them to expand and contract in response to the needs of the tissues they supply, by increasing or decreasing the flow of blood.

Tumour blood vessels break all of these rules. They rarely form the neat, hierarchical branching pattern found in normal tissues. Arteries can connect directly to veins without ever considering forming an intermediate capillary. Capillaries can develop into dead ends. The useful smooth muscle lining is often missing or, if present, does not function correctly. Large holes in vessel walls allow material and fluid to freely leak into the tumour tissue. Complex and tortuous branching patterns mean that blood flows sluggishly, often leading many areas of the tumour to chronically lack oxygen. However, cancer cells can adapt to thrive in these conditions, and those that develop the ability to live within their means and to manipulate their surroundings to optimise their chance of survival, can outcompete those that don't and, ultimately, those that comprise the rest of the body (which is, in part, why cancer can be deadly).

These observations of the contrast between normal and tumour blood vessels were the starting point for the growth processes we ultimately incorporated into *AitO*. Our prototype used computer simulations of blood vessel networks, based on a mathematical process known as a Lindenmayer system. Our simulation began with a single, large vessel, which at a certain distance along its length is branched into two smaller, narrower, vessels. Each of these daughter vessels was then divided into two smaller vessels, which were then also divided. The process was repeated for a predefined number of iterations until a detailed, multi-scale approximation of a blood vessel network was formed.[4] By controlling the angle defined between the branches and the relationship between the diameter and length of parent and daughter vessels, we were able to introduce an even greater level of realism.

4. Karshafian, R, PN Burns and MR Henkelman, "Transit time kinetics in ordered and disordered vascular trees", *Phys Med Biol*, 48, 19, 2003, pp. 3225–3237.

To simulate tumour blood vessels, the same simulation process was used, but with an element of randomness introduced into each of

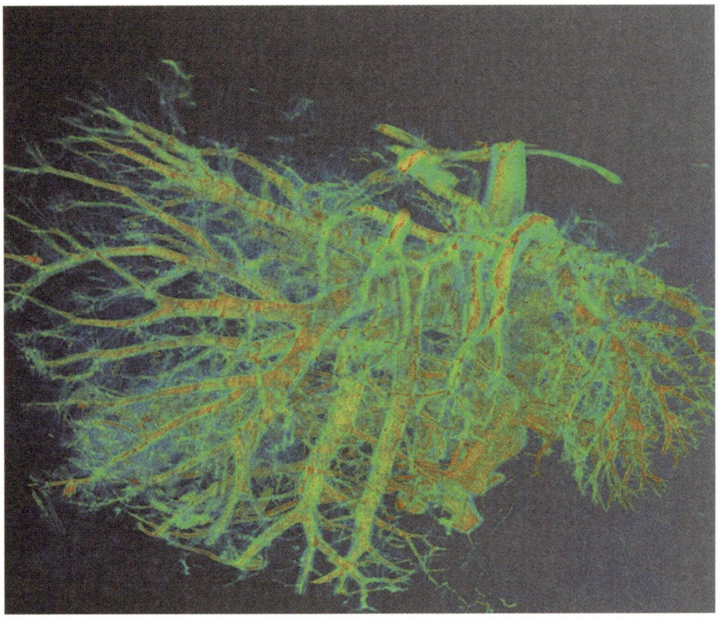

the parameters (vessel branching angle, diameter and length). During each branching step, a randomly generated number was added to the value associated with each daughter vessel, causing it to deviate from the 'perfect' branching pattern of the normal blood vessel network, resulting in a disorganised and chaotic structure, as shown in the images here. Indeed, in order to look realistic, the normal vessel networks also required a degree of randomness to be introduced, but in a much more constrained manner.

ABOVE Blood vessel network in a mouse liver, revealed using x-ray computed tomography, Jake Burrell.

The next stage of the project aimed to incorporate the dynamic processes of growth, angiogenesis, treatment and atrophy. My own day-to-day research aims to develop techniques for measuring characteristic elements of tumour physiology, such as blood flow and blood vessel leakiness, using MRI, and a key motivation for my work is to evaluate how well drugs can be delivered and how well they penetrate into tumours. In collaboration with researchers at the UCL Institute of Cancer, we have been investigating how tumours respond to novel drugs known as vascular disrupting agents (VDAs). VDAs target tumour vessels and cause them to collapse, thereby isolating the tumour from its vital supply of nutrients. We have been able to use our MRI scanner to detect this process occurring within hours of injecting the drug, which is a significant advancement over the normal assessment method that relies on the tumour shrinking in

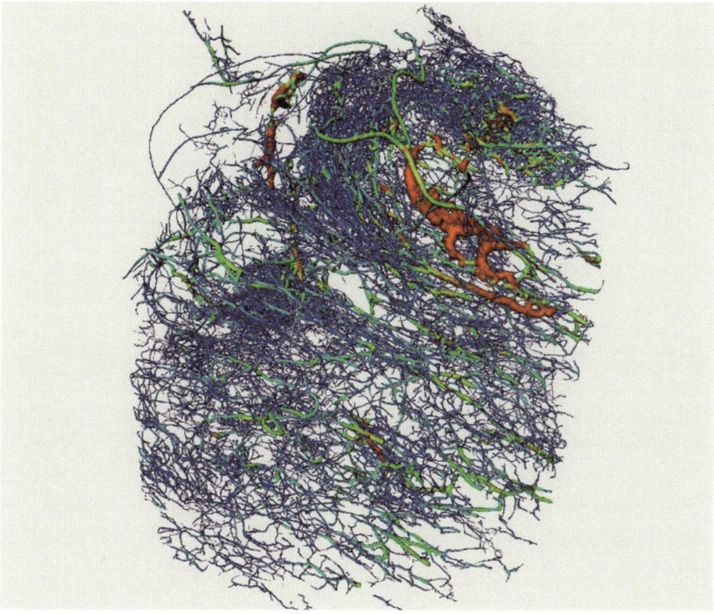

size (which can take weeks or months). However, it is also recognised that the inefficiencies associated with tumour blood supply, which we rely on to deliver drugs to the tumour, can cause treatment efficacy to be hindered.

To reflect these phenomena, a simulation in the form of a movie was constructed, in which simulated normal vessel networks were grown and then, at random points in the network, tumour growth was initiated. This second element of randomness had two key

ABOVE Three-dimensional rendering of blood vessels in a colorectal tumour, Jake Burrell.

components: first, the 'height' of the mutation within the normal vessel network dictated the 'severity' of the tumour, with mutation points occurring at larger branches going on to form larger tumours; second, it formed an analogy with the randomness of tumour formation at a genetic level. In the real world, for a real tumour to develop, mutations must occur in key genes (known as oncogenes) to enable the necessary characteristics to develop, such as the ability to replicate indefinitely. To develop such mutations are essentially random in nature, but must occur in parallel for a tumour to form (which takes a long time and is why cancer is usually a disease associated with old age). This was reflected in the randomness of the starting location of the tumour, and successful therapy was represented by a decay of tumour blood vessels and regrowth of normal blood vessels.

These relatively literal prototypes, which formed a foundation for Simeon Nelson and Nick Rothwell to abstract into the final version of the installation, have also filtered into my research work. Using very similar techniques to those used in the *AitO* prototypes, my research group is currently characterising patterns of tumour blood vessel networks from ultra-high resolution x-ray computed tomography (CT) scans, and comparing them with those found in normal tissues. Our goal is to characterise variations in blood flow within tumours that could also be detected using standard imaging approaches, and could help inform on regions within tumours that have limited inaccessibility to drugs. Moreover, my involvement with *AitO* allowed me to reflect on my experiences in studying tumour biology and biophysics and to further consider the nature of tumour blood vessels, and to consolidate my understanding of them. Science is an inherently creative discipline, but is highly constrained—the models and theorems that we create must accurately reflect an aspect of the universe that you are studying, otherwise it is invalid. Science-art collaborations remove these restrictions, and allow greater degree of personal expression.

Working on *AitO* also gave me the opportunity to talk about my work with cancer patients and gave me valuable insights into the view they may hold of my role as a scientist. These interactions made me think about the level of disconnection that can sometimes exist between scientists and patients, and of a view of scientists as detached and removed from what is feels like to experience cancer, on a personal level. We may sometimes be regarded by cancer patients as a faceless group, one step removed from the oncologists they regularly interact with, and therefore far removed from their own experience. This was specifically expressed by some patients, who were troubled by the positioning of cancer as a detached object of study, when it had so fundamentally and intimately affected their own lives. This contrasts with the day-to-day discussions I have about cancer, which are generally unemotional and detached, and so powerfully demonstrated the human aspect of the work that we, as scientists, undertake, and of the taboos and sensitivities associated with cancer that we can easily overlook.

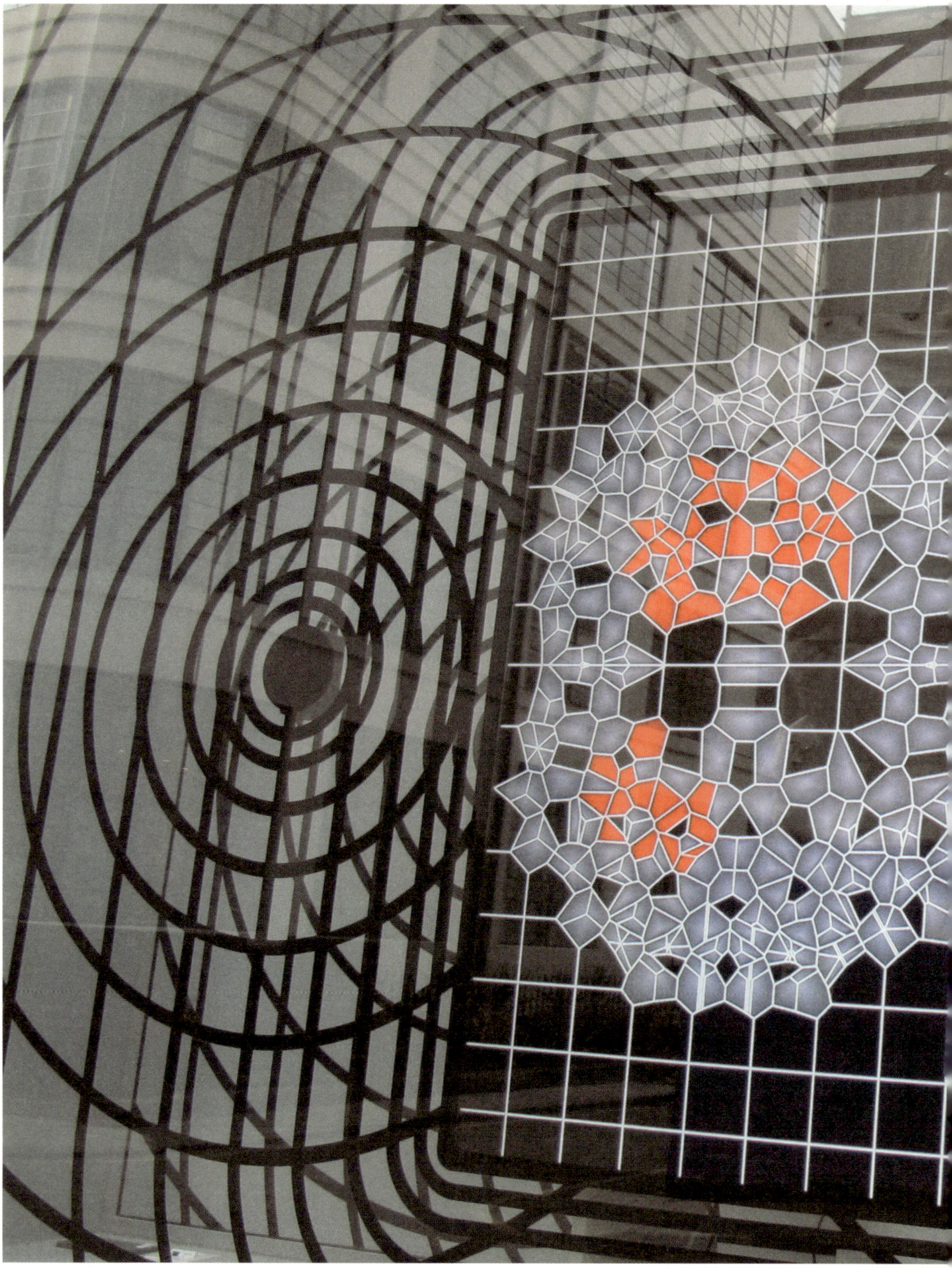

ABOVE Close-up view of installation in Capper Street windows. Photography Simeon Nelson.

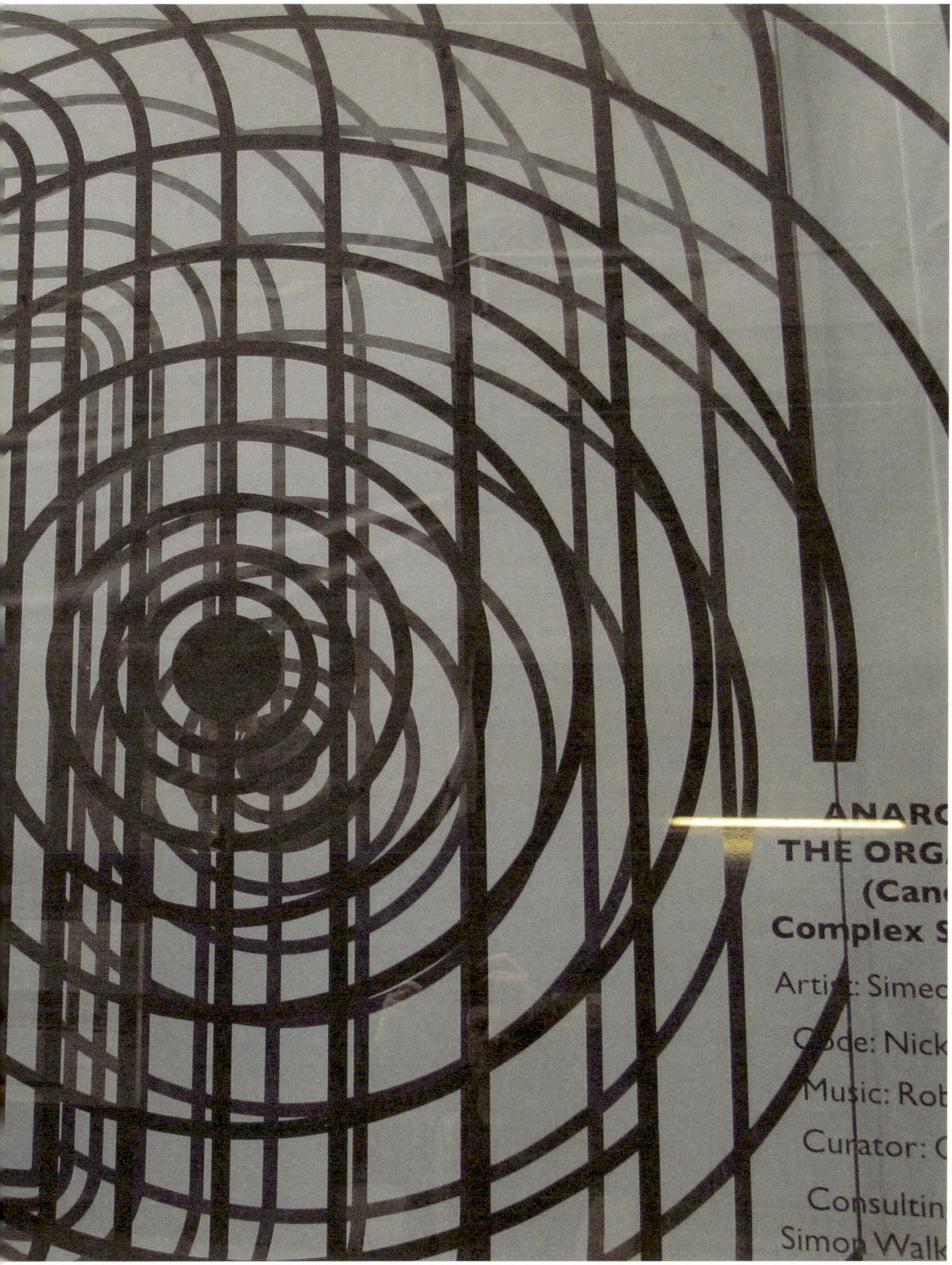
ANAR
THE ORG
(Can
Complex S
Arti : Sime
de: Nick
Mu ic: Rob
Cu ator:
Co sultin
Simo Walk

EXISTING IN-BETWEEN, LIMINAL AESTHETICS AND EMBODIED ETHICS

Monia Brizzi

'Cellular death sculpts our internal and external form.... We are, at every moment, partly dying and partly being reborn.'[1]

1. Ameisen, JC, "Dialogues entre la vie et la mort", *When Death Enters the Therapeutic Space: Existential Perspectives in Psychotherapy and Counselling*, L Barnett ed., East Sussex: Routledge, 2009.

'Art has a curative function in human experience when it reveals as in a flash intimate, absolute truth regarding the nature of things.'[2]

2. Whitehead, AN, *Adventures of Ideas*, Toronto: Collier-Macmillan, 1933.

'Art is the education of nature... a message from the unseen. It unlooses depths of feeling from behind the frontier where precision of consciousness fails.'[3]

3. Whitehead, *Adventures of Ideas*.

'Creativity achieves its supreme task of transforming disjointed multiplicity, with its diversities in opposition, into concrescent unity, with its diversities in contrast.'[4]

4. Whitehead, AN, *Process and Reality*, New York: The Free Press, 1929.

'The work of art allows repressed districts of the world and the soul to leave the ugly and enter into beauty.'[5]

5. Hillman, J, "The Practice of Beauty", *Uncontrollable Beauty: Towards a New Aesthetics*, B Beckley and D Shapiro eds, New York: Allworth Press, 1998.

'Death is the mother of beauty.'[6]

6. Stevens, W, *Sunday Morning*, 1915, quoted in May, R, *My Quest For Beauty*, Dallas, TX: Saybrook Publishing, 1985.

Health and illness have both natural-scientific and human-scientific aspects.[7] They also have aspects which precede and substantiate but entirely escape the scope of both types of science because despite being directly felt in a bodily and affective manner they are invisible, intangible, relational, ambiguous, unintentional, prereflective and nonverbal.

7. Teo, T, "Psychology Is Still a Problematic Science and the Public Knows It", *American Psychologist*, 67, 9, 2012.

These latter aspects constitute a sustaining border matrix that generates both the body and consciousness and yet is particularly hard to access precisely because in grounding, mediating and integrating them its hybrid liminal qualities are not gathered in a simple location but inhere everywhere. Being a middle or third dimension diffused between matter and mind implies that they cannot feasibly be fully given in, or boiled down to, either hard (the physicalist organism) or soft (the psyche) poles alone, for, as their middle, they exceed and withdraw the actualities of mere presence separate from potentiality.

The relational realism and deep empiricism of these fundamental and ubiquitous experiential structures of the threshold defy scientific representation but can be rescued through art. Art is the forming of the middle, that is, its carnal intelligibility.[8]

8. Hillman, J and M Ventura, *We've Had a Hundred Years of Psychotherapy and the World's Getting Worse*, New York: HarperCollins, 1992.

We are creatures of bio-chemistry, of psyche and of communication. Rather than being watertight compartments, these three dimensions consist of and partake of a relational amalgam or open form-in-process where all aspects incarnate, manifest and form/sculpt and are reciprocally incarnated in, manifested and formed/sculpted by one another.

The lived experience of being emerges at the interface between these several aspects. It manifests as the continual process of concrescent becoming and creative synthesis of their complementary impressions and expressions. It forms diffused unity out of multiplicity, contrasted harmony out of complexity, permanence out of flux, actuality out of potentiality, objectification out of transcendence, vitality out of perishing and situated freedom out of limitation.

The materiality of the constancy and stillness of physical and psychological substances is not inert stasis but process and change. Contingency, necessity and dissolution are the beginning of novel possibilities of being.

Life's cellular and psychosocial dimensions form a non-hierarchical and non-linear dynamic network to which they contribute their intrinsic-disjunctive (for their own sake) and relational-conjunctive (for the sake of the whole) significance: "It is not substance which is permanent, but form. Forms suffer changing relations; actual entities perpetually perish subjectively, but are immortal objectively"; they are "merely individual facts; and yet the good they did achieve in individual joy, in individual sorrow, in the introduction of needed contrast, is yet saved by its relation to the completed whole".[9]

9. Whitehead, *Process and Reality*, p. 346.

The "primitive form of physical experience is emotional"[10], and so the body is not a brute soulless object but one that is resonant and ensouled, and the psyche is not disembodied but incarnated in the body and through it also (situated) in the world. The psyche substantiates, feels and expresses the body and the body substantiates, senses and communicates the psyche. They are two inseparable forms of the same process, human life; two inseparable vantage points from which to view human life. Neither is a neutral or immune substance but is what it is according to how it is involved in the other, how it is formed/impressed/acted upon by the other and how it forms/expresses/acts upon that other.

10. Whitehead, *Process and Reality*, p. 162.

This implies that the experience of physical illness is not exhausted by the experience of the biological body as object but also stretches out to and affects the lived body's structural matrix of intra- and interpersonal relations: "First, there is affectivity, which assumes that the body *is* something other than a mathematical point and which gives it volume in space".[11]

11. Deleuze, G, *Bergsonism*, New York: Zone Books, 1966, p. 25.

Despite life's constitutional relational foundations and processual structures, our Western perspective divorces actuality from potentiality and is entrenched in the separatist logic of dualism and the fixed language of mere presence and static substance.

Indeed, both everyday and scientific practices are pervaded by unexamined assumptions and preconceived images that recognise but keep separate the dimensions of being and their links separate.[12] These assumptions structure and order not by integrating but by splitting the complexity of a living whole to which no further reference is made and dismissing "the baffling aspects of things into intellectual subordination… the easy road of Anaesthesia by which discordant factors are dismissed into irrelevance".[13]

12. Spinelli, E, "Relatedness, Uncertainty, and Anxiety: The Practice of Contemporary Psychotherapy", Institute of Physics, London, 19 January, 2013.

13. Whitehead, *Adventures of Ideas*, p. 47, p. 294.

While with Dynamic Systems Theory the physical sciences have in some areas begun to progress beyond deadening Newtonian dichotomy and abstraction, the social sciences and, in particular, psychology are still lagging behind and have not yet moved on enough from "clear-headed and narrow-visioned"[14] *either/or* substance essentialism to a more relational *both-and* stance, to the interactive process of physical and psychological substantiation.[15]

14. Whitehead, *Adventures of Ideas*, p. 48.

15. Spinelli, E, "Emphasising the Human in Psychotherapy", The Individual and Identity Conference, Association for Humanistic Psychology, London: 1 October 2011.

The insubstantiation of the hybrid and processual foundations of experience in the substance/process split breeds fragmentation, trivialises empirical reality and interferes with clinical and ethical relevance, for "in so far as there is trivial order, there must be trivialised actual entities"[16] and so "the methods of scientific psychology are inadequate for understanding experience".[17]

16. Whitehead, *Process and Reality*, p. 254.

17. Hollway, W, "Allowing Experience to Make Its Impact", Annual Conference Reports, *The Psychologist*, 25, 6, 2012, p. 427.

What makes sufferance even more difficult to live with is its "brute anaesthetised conception"[18] that separates it from its animating totality of affective involvements and significant relations. In doing so it encases sufferance in "abstract and empty concepts"[19] that fail to reflect its concretely lived actualities.

18. Hillman, J, *The Thought of the Heart and the Soul of the World*, New York: Spring Publications, 1992, p. 123. His emphasis.

19. Mølbak, RL, "From A Phenomenology of the Subject to a Phenomenology of the Event: Reconstructing the Ontological Basis for a Phenomenological Psychology", *Journal of Phenomenological Psychology*, 43, 2012, p. 209.

The traditional narrow focus of professional specialisation is problematic when it comes to health-care practice (rather than theory) because it disregards the fact that in practice the lived experience of health and illness is inescapably relationally diffused and liminal rather than gathered in a simple location, for "any aspect of relatedness inevitably impacts upon every aspect or expression of relatedness".[20]

20. Spinelli, E, *Practicing Existential Psychotherapy: The Relational World*, London: Sage, 2007, p. 20.

Human experience derives from a creative process of assembling heterogeneous elements into a complex, rather than unalloyed, unity, but "this doctrine, of the impossibility of tearing a proposition from its systematic context in the actual world"[21] runs counter to our Western desire for absolute power, to our rejection of liminality and limitation and to expertise's ambition to control and master reality instrumentally.

21. Whitehead, *Process and Reality*, p. 11.

Clearly professionalisation and expertise have several advantages, first among them the advancement of certain knowledgeable practices in society. But are their formal determinations and inventorised routines all we have? For they leave out the very important reality of many actual occasions of experience that factically materialise and enrich us.

Are our physical and psychosocial orders solely lacks of disorder? Is the solidity and solidarity of experience—that which concretises it the most—inert and inanimate? Is it simply the stable crystallisation of and staid exception to openness, movement and becoming? And are experience's processes merely insubstantial, immaterial and ephemeral?

Is illness simply lack of health, and health just the absence of illness and limitation? Are health and illness only physical or only psychological experiences? Are they only private and un-shareable? Or are they solely universal and predictable?

"[A]ll knowledge is either tacit or rooted in *tacit knowledge*. A wholly explicit knowledge is unthinkable".[22] If this is so, how can we access and express this primordial yet implicit, unspoken and unspeakable knowing?

22. Polanyi, M, "The Logic of Tacit Inference", *The Journal of the Royal Institute of Philosophy*, XLI (155), 1966, p. 7. His emphasis.

Given that different representations generate different understandings and mediate different experiences, what are the advantages of addressing cancer from an artistic perspective?

Works of art make available to immediate sense perception the pre-separated interrelational multidimensionality of life without displacing its acts and meanings into derivative clear-cut reports, fixed exegeses or valenced explanations that would diminish, oppose, finalise and ultimately explain them away. Artworks confront the standardised reporting and divided informancy of expertise with both the danger of their generalisations and the importance of their omissions, hence providing a "restraint upon specialists, and also an enlargement of their imaginations".[23]

23. Whitehead, *Process and Reality*, p. 17.

Art foregrounds what is otherwise suppressed, anaesthetised and ultimately alienated in conceptual systems of interpretation and representation so that it can emerge to life to address and be addressed by us. Art accesses the ordinarily inaccessible embodied structures of lived reality, speaks the otherwise unspeakable, visualises the previously invisible and makes possible the otherwise impossible.

By responding to "the need to bring to language modes of being that ordinary vision obscures or even represses"[24], art is much more than mere luxury, embellishment, frivolity, distraction or even escapism from more serious concerns. It grants the unmediated disclosure of commonly hidden aspects of embodied experience. It enables us to feel their tensions and make sense of them in a personally engaged way through the sensorial-sensuous experience of being bodily, emotionally and spiritually affected and called into activity, into question and into perceptivity by the *pathic* qualities of the artwork to offer a personally committed response.

24. Ricoeur, P, Interpretation Theory: Discourse and the Surplus of Meaning, 1976, discussed in Hustwit, JR, "Is Recoeur a Process Philosopher? Interpretation and Becoming", *Process Studies*, 37, 1, 2008.

In experiencing a work of art we are invited, involved, seized, exposed, touched, moved, stricken and transformed beyond (the limits of) words, beyond preset determinations, beyond the self-referential parameters of specialist expertise, and beyond the inflated detachment of *gnostic* rationality which, unchallenged and unsupplemented, is "in effect a form of anti-rationalism", an "arbitrary halt to a particular sent of abstractions".[25]

25. Whitehead, AN, *Science and the Modern World*, New York: The Free Press, 1925, p. 201.

In speaking and interpellating the language of lived experience, art calls directly upon our embodied activity and personal commitment, and offers unmediated access to that which is otherwise reactive, dissociated, neglected, unqualified—ethically uncompelling and unseised.

The "actual cannot be reduced to mere matter of fact in divorce from the potential"[26], and so the liminal territories prior to conventional substance/process, subject/object and order/chaos splits are reflectively vague and conceptually indeterminate despite being really primal and basic. They are primordially forming and being formed in our ongoing experience of being: "transcendence does not consist of objectification but *objectification presupposes transcendence*".[27]

26. Whitehead, *Process and Reality*, p. 227.

27. Heidegger in May, R, *The Discovery of Being*, New York: Norton & Company, 1983, p. 149. His emphasis.

We simply don't have the words to capture the form of their elusive yet concrete materiality in a certain fully formed way[28]; we don't have names to name the unnameable. These liminal territories are the *heart of the matter* of significance and value, a *fact* yet not matter-of-fact—incommensurably in the midst of substance and process. Finding a structure that is empirically, clinically and ethically effective in expressing this primary totality requires liberating rather than assimilating the substantiating constancy of existence's transience, contrast and finitude.

28. Spinelli, "Relatedness, Uncertainty, and Anxiety: The Practice of Contemporary Psychotherapy".

The simultaneously concrete *and* ineffable, actual *and* potential, unified *and* contrasted, static *and* processual reality of the whole cannot be entirely present-at-hand and spatialised. It is not given in representation but is able to overflow and stand revealed in structural concretion only insofar as this "is essentially open onto a totality that is itself open".[29] It is a matter of securing by insecuring and solving by dissolving certainty and sedimentation.

29. Deleuze, *Bergsonism*, p. 105.

Throughout time, human beings have sought a structure to tap into and express the more foundational and embodied qualities of being, but in this quest they have confused things even more. With a misplaced emphasis on representation, logos and language, they have constructed lofty and barely decipherable intellectual highways that can all too often only be understood by a specific niche of experts, such as in the specialist jargon of science, philosophy and psychotherapy.

If expression does not speak to lived experience it gives it no meaning. It annihilates lived experience by leaving it unattended, unaddressed and unformed, tacit in the recesses of private experience. If communication is gnostic rather than pathic, if it is analytical, detached and divisive rather than sensorial, involved and unified, it reduces life to formalised instances which then require more compensatory subjectivist fantasies or unqualified universalisms to bridge and re-animate the wasteland that divides presumed meaning from actual felt experience.

The reconciling structures of *Anarchy in the Organism* eschew the conventions of a linguistic tradition so as to interfere with the grammar's homogenous rule, suspend its determinacy, and allow something that is obscured—something primordial—to surface.[30] The structures in this book enable the processual complementarity and disproportion of existential dwelling *in-between* irreconcilabilities to be at last actively encountered and appropriated in a thoroughly embodied and emancipatory manner. The book's *veritas aesthetica* makes visible and audible the tensions inherent in the structure of intelligibility, letting them speak directly to bodily sensate perception. Aesthetic pathic undergoing grounds and informs the secondary and retroactive verbalisations of gnostic knowing; it is their humus but remains unexhausted by them.

30. Hustwit, "Is Ricoeur a Process Philosopher? Interpretation and Becoming", p. 66.

In challenging and inverting the Wittgensteinian bias that "whereof one cannot speak, thereof must one be silent", *Anarchy in the Organism* delivers us from the continual bumping of our heads against the constricting walls of language, revealing that there *is* much more to life than our rationalisations, conceptual categorisations and verbal distillations.

Veritas logica with its fixation on brute substance and its cognitive strictures, protective defences and calculative hubris for precision and control all too often lure us to overlook that "the capacity to speak is founded on the capacity of the cosmos to signify.... The revealing grounds the saying, not the reverse."[31]

In presenting rather than representing and in showing but not explaining, *Anarchy in the Organism* challenges the nihilistic and dehumanising supposition that "mankind has consciously entertained all the fundamental ideas which are applicable to its experience" and that "human language, in single words or in phrases" can "explicitly express these ideas".[32]

31. Ricoeur, P, *Interpretation Theory: Discourse and the Surplus of Meaning*, 1976, discussed in Hustwit, "Is Ricoeur a Process Philosopher? Interpretation and Becoming", pp. 62-63.

32. Whitehead, AN, *Modes of Thought*, New York: The Free Press, 1938, p. 173.

Hence this artwork confronts the epistemological, clinical and ethical violence[33] of interpreting life in ways that diminish and powerfully redirects emphasis from certain but anaesthetised self-contained units to the reverberating border aesthetics of liminal relations and "full-fledged human experience".[34] The book's aesthetic and relational ethics brings into corporeal intelligibility life's foundational in-betweenness, the primal liminality that is the bedrock of both the original Greek conception of truth as *aletheia* (an animating unfinalised openness to being rather than correspondence or accuracy) and of Dynamic Systems Theory in science (where the more it is known the less this is predictable or setteable in any knowledge way).[35]

33. Teo, T, "From Speculation to Epistemological Violence in Psychology: A Critic-Hermeneutic Reconstruction", *Theory and Psychology*, 18, 1, 2008.

34. Mølbak, "From A Phenomenology of the Subject to a Phenomenology of the Event: Reconstructing the Ontological Basis for a Phenomenological Psychology", p. 189.

35. Spinelli, "Relatedness, Uncertainty, and Anxiety: The Practice of Contemporary Psychotherapy".

In illness and in art we occupy a *no longer-not yet*[36] of radical disclosure where we are actively transformed but not "in control" and where we become able not only to put up with or adapt to these experiences but also to grow through them much more by letting go of than by holding on to certainties and masteries that we might justifiably claim but, alas, do not *really* experience.

36. Heidegger, M, *Being and Time*, Malden, MA: Blackwell Publishing, 1927.

The experience of both illness and art shows us that what is most real, substantial, vital and important in our lives is made not *by* us but *through* and *for* us[37] and that it is possible to "become different through an experience and not simply remain its unfettered master".[38]

37. Hillman and Ventura, *We've Had a Hundred Years of Psychotherapy and the World's Getting Worse*.

38. Mølbak, "From A Phenomenology of the Subject to a Phenomenology of the Event: Reconstructing the Ontological Basis for a Phenomenological Psychology", p. 187.

Anarchy in the Organism re-embeds cancer in wider life-sustaining processes in mental and physical life and in the natural and cultural orders. By challenging the individualistic closing-in of illness and the privatisation of death—and by opening them onto balanced intensities of systemic participation—the artwork avoids reflecting and perpetuating the cellular splits and fundamentalist metastases that characterise cancer.

What mostly makes us real is not of our own making but assails us from "inside", from "outside", from "above", letting us realise who we are in meanings and events and what they are in us only after the fact, after they have already and unexpectedly happened—that is, after they have already acted upon and changed us in ways we don't yet know and before we can reciprocally act upon and influence them in return.[39] Our agency is finite and our mastery is at best blinkered and provisional.

39. See Mølbak, "From A Phenomenology of the Subject to a Phenomenology of the Event: Reconstructing the Ontological Basis for a Phenomenological Psychology", p. 187.

Anarchy in the Organism expands mainstream *subject or hero centred* humanistic and empiricist accounts of (calculative) intentionality to include those primary instances where we are not in control of or manipulating experience but are taken over by it and "intentionality is inverted. I become the objective of the object"[40], where I can grasp experiences only on the basis of their having already grasped me, where I am constituted by events in their act of addressing/sculpting me that summons me to address/sculpt them in return and thereby become each other's subject/impression, object/expression and "*artistic medium*".[41]

40. Marion, J, *The Erotic Phenomenon*, 2007, discussed in Mølbak, "From A Phenomenology of the Subject to a Phenomenology of the Event: Reconstructing the Ontological Basis for a Phenomenological Psychology".

41. Brown, S and P Stenner, *Psychology Without Foundations: History, Philosophy and Psychosocial Theory*, London: Sage, 2009, p. 201.

In speaking directly to our felt bodily experiences, *Anarchy in the Organism* provides a participatory and emancipatory aesthetic ethics

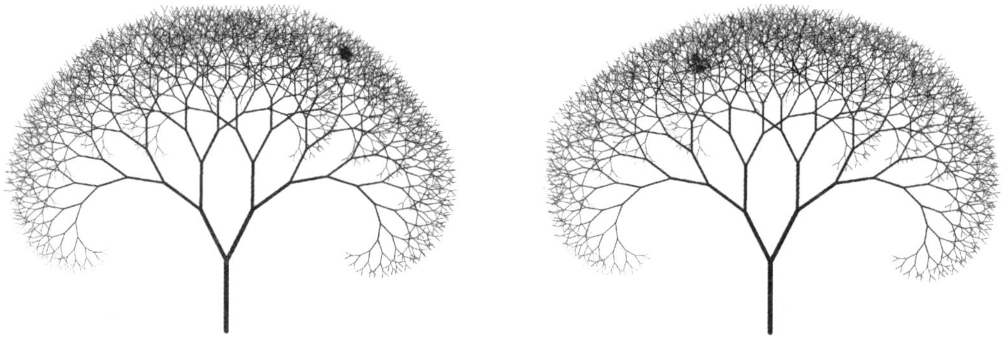

that appreciates and redeems baffling elements, tensions and contradictions from neglect and repression, and that enables us to enter into conversational familiarity with and take responsibility for the constituting materials of our immediate carnal experience of being.

In linking the mind and the heart to the world, as well as physical-psychological and personal-collective dimensions, and in bringing subordinated elements to the forefront of medical care, *Anarchy in the Organism* challenges inequality and marginalisation, one-way knowledge and the cult of expertise, advances "concientisation"[42], social reflexivity and collaborative knowledge creation. It enriches

42. Murray, M and R Gray, "Health Psychology and the Arts: A Conversation", *Journal of Health Psychology*, 13, 2, 2008.

ABOVE Tumour blood vessel diagrams showing a tumorous growth, Simon Walker-Samuel.

scientific understandings of what it means to be and to suffer, breathing life into and humanising the "traditional emphasis on problem solving" and "deficit discourse" of healthcare practice.[43]

43. Gergen, K, *Relational Being: Beyond Self and Community*, New York: Oxford University Press, 2009, pp. 328-329.

This empowering work of art nourishes the creativity and "emotional vitality central to ethical knowing".[44] It deepens our receptivity, responsiveness and capacity to care to make sense, to create meaning and to hold, integrate and transform the paradoxical and conflictual, the senseless and the meaningless.[45]

44. Hollway, "Allowing Experience to Make Its Impact".

45. Galvin, K and L Todres, *Caring and Well-being: A Lifeworld Approach*, Abingdon, Oxon: Routledge, 2013.

Anarchy in the Organism sensitises our Western divided perspective and its subjugation of pathic values, relatedness, complexity, uncertainty and finitude by opening it up to the ethical engagement and existential zest of fully embodied and single-hearted commitment, unconditional affirmation and *amor fati*. In its reconciliatory horizons struggle and grace and perishing and becoming

> 'are not opposites so much as they are polar qualities which call forth each other. As the individual's scope of sensitivity becomes enlarged, bringing a wider range of responsiveness, so also does the

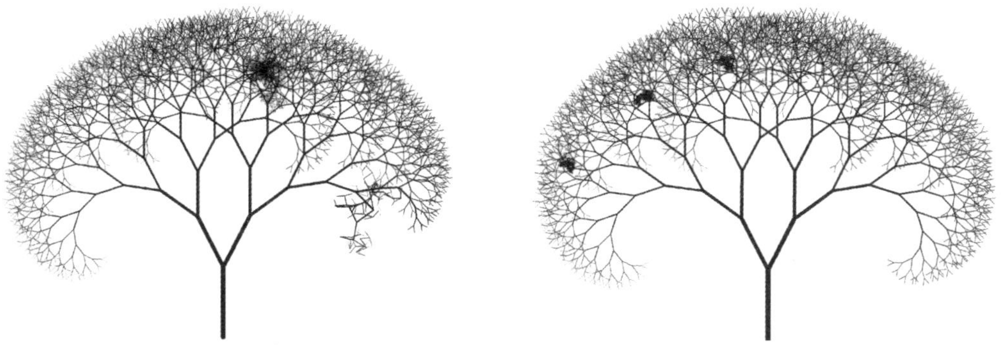

> pain and suffering deepen. The baffling ambiguity of life inheres in the impossibility of disjoining these contrasts without serious loss in complexity and intensity of value. For once permanence is abstracted from flux and lifted to dominance in awareness, the complexity of the present moment is simplified and its intensity diluted just as surely as by elevating the flux of passing values to dominant emphasis, disjoined from that which abides. Likewise, the notion of freedom unbounded by necessity of some sort, or of necessity which forecloses any exercise of even a modicum of freedom, confronts life with unlivable antinomies'.[46]

46. Frankenberry, N, "The Empirical Dimension of Religious Experience", *Process Studies* 8, 4, 1978.

ABOVE Tumour blood vessel diagrams showing a tumorous growth, Simon Walker-Samuel.

COMPLEXITY, HETEROGENEITY AND MEDICINE

Jorge Castillo-Sepúlveda & Francisco Tirado

When we refer to biomedical sources of information about cancer, we usually find definitions like this: "Cancer is a condition where cells in a specific part of the body grow and reproduce uncontrollably", or, "Cancer is a term used for diseases in which abnormal cells divide without control and are able to invade other tissues. Cancer cells can spread to other parts of the body through the blood and lymph systems."[1] From both definitions we may deduce that cancer is a process which is located and takes place in a body, that is, it has an existence of its own; cancer is an entity, it is recognised as something situated in a particular time and space, according to a conceptual framework which embraces a variety of activities or practices. We can expect that the system of activities predominantly linked to cancer is the biomedical, a work scheme that aligns biological knowledge and clinical practices in a new technoscientific field.[2]

1. National Health System, Information on cancer anduseful links" in *NHS Choices Your health, your choices.* 25 June 2012, viewed on 17 August 2012; National Cancer Institute, "Defining cancer" in *National Cancer Institute*, 2 June 2012, viewed on 18 August 2012, http://www.cancer.gov/cancertopics/cancerlibrary/what-is-cancer.

2. Cambrosio, A, P Keating and P Bourret, "Regulatory objectivity and tests systems in medicine: The case of cancerology", *Convergencia. Revista de Ciencias Sociales*, no. 42, September December 2006, pp. 121-139.

With his installation *Anarchy in the Organism* (*AitO*), Simeon Nelson has offered a visual and in-motion perspective on life as an unpredictable phenomenon. Cancer is certainly unpredictable. It can be considered as an expression of the instability of life itself, but also as a kind of particular material and social assemblage. For its expression is not reduced to biology, but has social and natural aspects of disorganisation that could be considered as deviations immanent in the thing itself. In various senses, cancer is aligned with several fields in the sociology and anthropology of medicine. In such research the phenomenon of cancer and its connections are shown to interweave with different domains, an interweaving which makes it somewhat more complex than the definitions above might suggest.[3]

3. Cambrosio, A, et al., "Mapping the emergence and development of translational cancer research", *European Journal of Cancer*, 42, 18, 2006, pp. 3140–3148.

The work of the Group for Social Studies in Science and Technology addresses cancer as a biomedical object, considering it as both a material and a social assemblage. Our investigation has been developed within the field of science and technology studies, a research area derived from the sociology of scientific knowledge, which is now a transdisciplinary space. Our participation in *AitO* intends to give an account of the complex organisation of cancer and how it becomes something different from its traditional conception in the biomedical field. In this account we emphasise the complexity of oncological practices. Ultimately, our intention is to show how the disease shifts into domains that transcend the body and is situated at various scales and spaces.

For several theorists, complexity is highly dependent on heterogeneity and how it is articulated. For example, Edgar Morin, philosopher and sociologist, assumes that the basis of a scope on complexity is the product of multiple interactions between markedly different entities.[4] This refers to how different elements interact with each other, forming a dynamic field of materials and relations. If we take a conventional approach to an event, we may assume a linear progression and the possibility of reducing components that are part of certain reactions (explanation as definition of cause). From the perspective of complexity, however, what is conceived as linear is necessarily recursive (consequences that are causes) and is composed of heterogeneous formations that interact reciprocally. Thus, to explain something is to situate it in a plane, that is, to offer a perspective in which different aspects of a thing, which we might identify as 'entities', exist at the same level, indicating their mutual relationships.[5] The emphasis on diversity requires, above all, conceiving each aspect as a unique strength, each one in relation to others. It is what Bruno Latour has noted as irreducibility: "There is no thing itself that is reducible or irreducible to any other", offering the chance of understanding how several entities are related and constitute assemblies of a socio-material order.[6]

4. Morin, E, *On Complexity*, New York: Hampton Press, 2008.

5. As it is noted in a etymological dictionary: "[Explain comes] from *explanationem* ( ), noun of action from ( ) *explanare* to make plain or clear, explain"': D Harper, Explanation (n.), in *Online Etymology Dictionary*, 2012, viewed on 17 August 2012, http://www.etymonline.com/index. php?term= explanation.

6. Latour, B, *The pasteurization of France*, Cambridge, MA.: Harvard University Press, 1988, p. 158.

Biomedicine has transformed the way we understand the phenomenon of life. It has established new diagrams for approximation from the integration of different material and social orders. We consider that there are two axes that very generally allow us to understand these modes of affection. The first one is related to what Nikolas Rose calls the molecularisation of life itself.[7] According to Rose, biomedicine has varied scales of life, offering a new working position that lies at the genetic or molecular level. It offers not only the possibility of new chains of association for explaining the phenomena of life, but also the possibilities of life's transformation: the object of biomedicine, then, is not so much the pathological as scope for intervention, but normality as an opportunity for optimisation. Heterogeneity links different scales, while molecularisation reorganises diverse actors and their relationships: institutions, policies, large-scale economic investment and scientific culture must all be transformed to enable vision and intervention on life at this level.

7. Rose, N, *The Politics of Life Itself*, Princeton: Princeton University Press, 2007.

The second axis refers to the ways in which this heterogeneity is manifested. Several authors have noted that, in the biomedical field, there is a logic behind what has been called "evidence-based medicine".[8] They say that this shows an authentic management of technoscientific work, from the production of tests, processing of results and evaluation of means, and that from it entities can be identified that interact with them. This interaction involves both regulation as a way to produce objectivity, and the need for an objectivity that is mediated by regulation. They have called this

8. For example, Cambrosio, et al., "Regulatory objectivity and tests systems in medicine: The case of cancerology."

reciprocal interaction "regulatory objectivity"; it implies that entities that are part of biomedical activities arise through technical and technological means, which participate in its description, and, at the same time, regulations that act for it. Both processes, molecularisation and regulatory objectivity, would be part of the reframing of biomedical activity in recent times. Science and technology studies have paid attention to these changes and have offered new frameworks for their understanding. In particular, Actor-Network Theory (also called Symmetrical Sociology or Sociology of Associations) has offered alternative ways to do this. This perspective assumes the participation of heterogeneous entities in a same level—flat perspective—for the constitution of events that addresses human or non-human alike. Thus, biomedical objects result from the production of complex relationships, whose meaning can be located or described in a plane. However, the meaning "is taken in its original non-textual and nonlinguistic interpretation: how one privileged trajectory is built, out of an infinite number of possibilities", which leads us to try to account for how different actors or actants are both part of and constitute these trajectories.[9]

9. Akrich, M and B Latour, "A Summary of a Convenient Vocabulary for the Semiotics of Human and Nonhuman Assemblies", *Shaping Technology, Building Society. Studies in Sociotechnical Change*, J Law and W Bijker, eds, Cambridge, MA: Massachusetts Institute of Technology, 1992, p. 259.

For this, and in what refers to cancer, we developed a case study from focused ethnographies, in-depth interviews with patients and professionals, and the analysis of various medical guidelines—OncoGuides—or protocols developed by the Catalan Agency for Health Information, Assessment and Quality (AATRM).[10] This has been facilitated by the cooperation of the Association of Breast Cancer Patients, gAmis (Grup d'Ajuda Mama Salut).[11] The orientation of this research has been to address the meaning of cancer, maintaining the symmetry principle that has advocated the Actor-Network Theory. According to it, this principle should be integrated into a single explanation or description, both the social and material components of a situation, trying to give an account of the agencies distributed in a network of relations. In this sense, we try to clarify what cancer means, and we do it from three approaches. The first refers to its meaning based on reports of breast cancer patients and oncologists. The second refers to how different technoscientific mediations affect how cancer is embodied or experienced in the body. The latter provides a conceptual framework to apprehend these approaches. The meaning of cancer from patient and professional accounts is articulated as trajectory. In other words, heterogeneous materials and processes compose cancer as a path between different actors and events. We would like to realise this idea from the following extract of an interview with a patient:

10. Knoblauch, H, "Focused ethnography", *Forum: Qualitative Social Research*, 6, 3, 2005, viewed on 12 February 2010, ; AATRM, Published clinical practice guidelines, AATRM, 2 February 2012, viewed on 13 March 2010, http://www.gencat.cat/salut/depsan/units/aatrm/html/en/dir398/doc13552.html.

11. Webpage may be consulted at http://www.gamisassociacio.org

> Because really for anyone diagnosed, the hardest time begins when you're diagnosed and lasts until you walk into the circuit. It is quite certain [when] they say [to] you, 'watch this', mammography, biopsy, *isa carcinoma*, whatever, will have to operate or start treatment, you have to do analytical, plaque, electro, pre-operative, have to go to.... You start a circuit, but this circuit is maybe 15, 20 days or a month, until you operate. At that time you are disconnected from what is breast cancer.[12]

12. Patient No. 8, personal interview, 25 October 2011.

The varying accounts of cancer articulate the platform of biomedical oncology. They link different biological, technical and social scales. Besides the biological body, other processes are involved in the definition of the disease. Here, the manifestation of cancer as an event in the life history of patients depends on a number of other actors that constitute it, in turn, as the association of various aspects and how they blend together through their engagement in the course of the disease. Understanding the meaning of cancer involves accounting for these actors, be they doctors, assistants, diagnostic tests, preparatory procedures, periodic evaluations, among many others. This trajectory is not necessarily

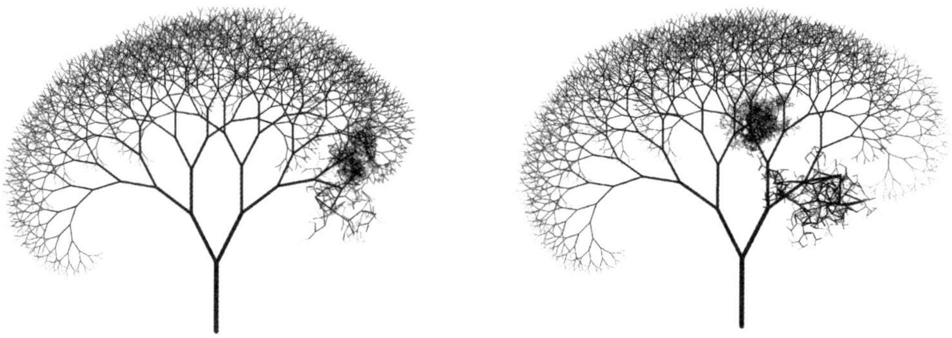

linear, because the results of a test can be used both for diagnosis and for the foundation of an intervention, and this one, at the same time, to specify a diagnosis. Thereby, beyond a meaning as a linear or local process, there are references to kinds of activity that reorder the notion of time and space. Time, because it is closely linked to the biomedical actions and tests; the material sense of present and future is engaged with the type of result produced by them. Space, because both material and semiotic elements are reordered to "produce the disease" or the mode in which it emerges in the social and technical fabric. Graphically, this could be expressed in the form of a field of mutually influencing relationships that affect the configuration adopted by all actors.[13]

13. Although the interpretation is a variant property, see Lockhart Nelson, S, Cut vinyl pattern, in *Anarchy in the organism*, 1 March 2012, viewed on 29 August 2012.

ABOVE Tumour blood vessel diagrams showing a tumorous growth, Simon Walker-Samuel.

In relation to how cancer is embodied, this process results are highly dependent on technoscientific mediations, which pronounce it as a disease and promote some kind of treatment. The entities that are part of the trajectories of cancer are strongly associated with several regulatory activities that enact and put in relation different scales, times and spaces. This means that cancer is composed of a variety of elements that go beyond the body itself and distribute the disease in a number of socio-material entities. For example, the following quote shows how a patient conceives the experience of the disease process in her body:

> I have had cancer, look what I say, I've had, and I didn't feel pain, all the damage to me [has] been done by them, to heal something that I have not seen, that did not hurt and I didn't feel. So that's the situation. Because someone saw a picture of I do not know what, they have done to me.... And they have made me happen.... But I didn't feel anything before.[14]

14. Patient No. 2, personal interview, 16 June 2011.

Instead of referring to their own body and a perceived change in it, many patients rely primarily on the biomedical network as a resource that organises their experience and gives meaning to the alterations

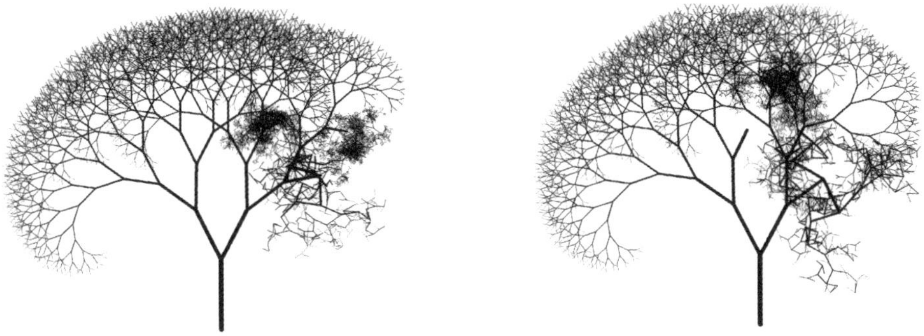

they may have suffered. The process on (in) the body cannot be thought of without several epistemic and material elements that enable a particular medical approach to the disease. In this order, certain molecular (genetic) categories enact anticipatory practices, which make the disease present even without the abnormal growth or division of cells.[15] With regard to the collectives involved in the process, expertise is located in the clinical groups responsible for the preparation of evidence, recommendations and guidelines. These are conditions of possibility of local clinical activity. In this context, regulation enables the articulation between different spatial and temporal domains. It doesn't act as a homogenisation process, but is the base for production

15. Castillo, J, F Tirado and M Rosengarten, "A symmetrical approach to mammal cancer: heterogeneity, regulation and embodiment", *Athenea Digital*, in press.

ABOVE Tumour blood vessel diagrams showing a tumorous growth, Simon Walker-Samuel.

systems of evidence and schemes of reflexivity of the practice itself, through: (a) diagnostic categories, which are product of specific techniques; (b) the possibility of mobilisation of several components between different centres of a health-care network, which affect spatiality itself (e.g., specialists, equipment and packages of tests); (c) a type of special relationship between specialists and such guidelines or evidence systems. With respect to the latter, the specialist takes a set of qualities and potential through the Onco Guides, without losing their identity. This kind of relation has been named "prehension", remembering the notion developed by Alfred North Whitehead.[16] The protocols and guidelines, as noted, are more than procedural rules and routines; they constitute the materiality of the definition of cancer and the representation that the specialists have on it. In the biomedical field, cancer cannot be thought of without its protocols. Cancer is an object that is accounted as a trajectory, being highly articulated with regulations and conventions and which presents particular temporal and spatial dimensions. Its materiality expresses qualities, which expands its presence through different spatial temporal conditions, beyond the body. We consider that the heterogeneity of

16. Tirado, F, and J Castillo, "Oncoguides-ontoguides: protocols, panoramas and prehension in cancer treatment, *Athenea Digital*, 11, 1, 2011, pp. 129–154; Whitehead, AN, *Process and reality. An essay in cosmology*, New York: Free Press, 1979.

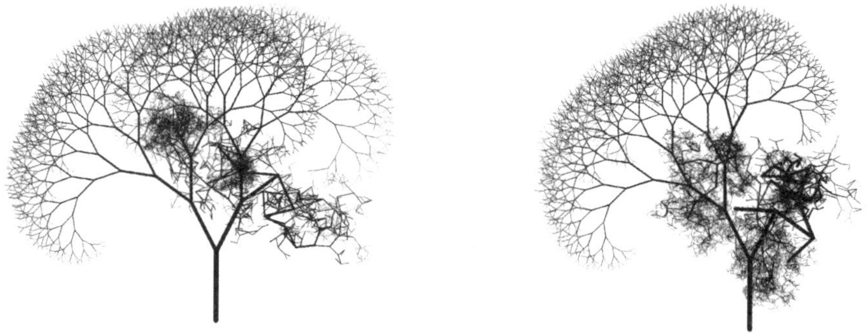

scales, spaces and times involved in the pathways of cancer can be understood from what the philosopher AN Whitehead conceptualised as "potentiality".[17] A "potential" object is a ubiquitous, efficient and entirely present entity. This means that it is not confined to a specific location, influencing and being influenced by the relationships that constitute it as a "present" object. For Whitehead, it is an error to assume that anything that is real must have a simple spatial location. At the same time, it is a mistake to consider that concrete entities are more real than extensional relations as genuine deliverances of experience.[18] His proposal is to problematise traditional categories of thought that place objects only as discrete and local. Unlike Aristotelian and scholastic philosophy that sees potency as a state,

17. Whitehead, *Process and reality: an essay in cosmology.*

18. Herstein, G, "Alfred North Whitehead (1861–1947)", ***Encyclopaedia of Philosophy***, 8 May 2007, viewed on 12 February 2012, http://www.iep.utm.edu/whitehed/.

ABOVE Tumour blood vessel diagrams showing a tumorous growth, Simon Walker-Samuel.

something that reaches its perfection to be present, for Whitehead, 'potential' is related to the situation, but is not limited to any location, being its main features efficiency and ubiquity.[19] A 'potential' expresses "at all points one definite physical fact".[20] An analogy, which might help to describe it, is a gravitational field: it is not reduced to a location (ubiquity) and affects how entities organise themselves and with each other; at the same time it remains completely present. We believe that understanding the disease in this way shifts the discussion of cancer to a level where both the social and the material become important, and we consider it is aligned with the proposal of *AitO* also. Anarchy is a kind of political disposition in which there is no formal or exclusive sovereign. In that sense, disorder is a kind of assemblage or order in which all the entities have similar quantum of participation on it. The same happens in a 'potential', in the sense of Whitehead: it is not a discrete and unique object, but one that is constituted by heterogeneity, and there are some political implications of the disease conceived as it. For example, the limits and the possibilities of affection by the disease are not linked only to the process in the body, nor on the body. It is—and it is necessary—complex assemblage with the body, i.e., several

19. Stengers, I, *Thinking with Whitehead. A free wild creation of concepts*, Cambridge, MA.: Harvard University Press, 2011.

20. Herstein, "Alfred North Whitehead (1861–1947)", p. 36.

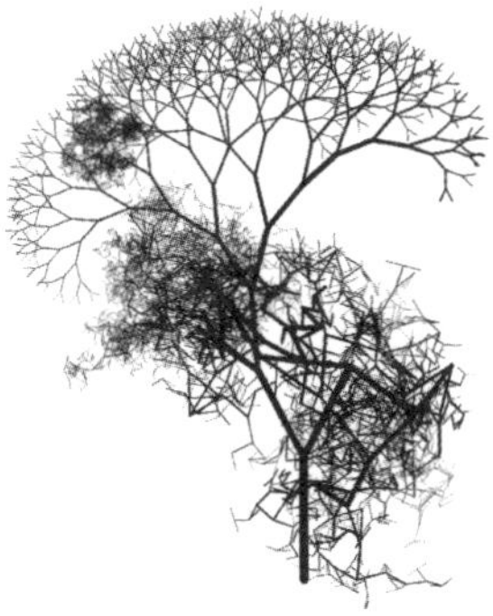

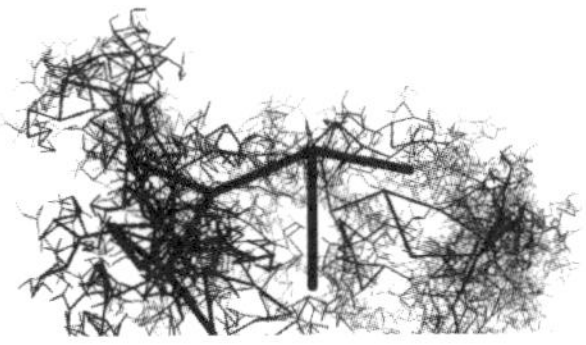

actors are articulated and make the presence of disease in some way. This produces a determined kind of body itself, e.g., a 'potential' and 'potentially' body that carries genetic possibility to develop a disease. At the same time, 'potential' involves all of us. Cancer as a 'potential' engages us in several ways in our everyday life. Thus, it is necessary to consider how not only individuals and families are part of the process, but also how a complex of materials, meanings and dissemination of biomedical knowledge by various means, participate on it. It is a path that involves a transformation in the lifestyles—or how to live with or without cancer, how it is regulated and how it is prevented—and thus, how life is organised itself.

ABOVE Tumour blood vessel diagrams showing a tumorous growth, Simon Walker-Samuel.

NOTES ON THE MUSIC

Rob Godman

Simeon asked me to create the music for this project only a year after my Dad had died of cancer. Having worked on previous projects with Simeon and Nick, I was confident we could deal with the subject matter in a way that would reflect the enormity of cancer on humanity to some extent, investigate our interests in arts/science and reflect on my own sensitivities and personal feelings towards cancer at the time. Our work often includes high-end technology and science models. There may be a (false) perception that such technology hides the 'human' and the 'personal'. For us all, *Anarchy in the Organism* is very, very personal....

There are currently two versions of *Anarchy in the Organism*—an algorithmic version installed at the University College Hospital Macmillan Cancer Centre, London (the work features four simultaneous algorithmic video projections and octophonic 'whispering windows' audio diffusion) and a live 'concert-hall' version for Eb clarinet, Live & Algorithmic Sound Projection and Responsive Video (written for the clarinettist Kate Romano).

The video animations are closely modelled on Voronoi cell systems with tumours growing amidst the organisms causing systemic collapse. These algorithms are based on venous network geometries supplied by Simon Walker-Samuel, senior research associate at the Centre for Advanced Biomedical Imaging at UCH.

Initially, I had investigated using the same biological models to create the sound for this work—it was the most obvious thing to do, the technology we use could have made sense of the data and 'converted' it into sound. But somehow it seemed to avoid the issue of what *Anarchy in the Organism* is all about—the appalling contradiction between the apparent beauty and self-destructive strength of the cancerous cellular growth and the affect of the cancer on the sufferer and their families. Therefore, the music became more organic in its approach with the idea of multi-layered duality and interaction becoming increasingly important.

The music for *Anarchy in the Organism* exploits our perception of time. I love the fact that machines are able to measure time incredibly accurately, yet human perception of time is deeply inaccurate and dependant on emotion and physiological matters. Central to the concept is the idea of interruption, interference and disturbance—all elements that are analogous to the introduction of a cancerous cell into a system. The music uses a rhythmic technique I am calling

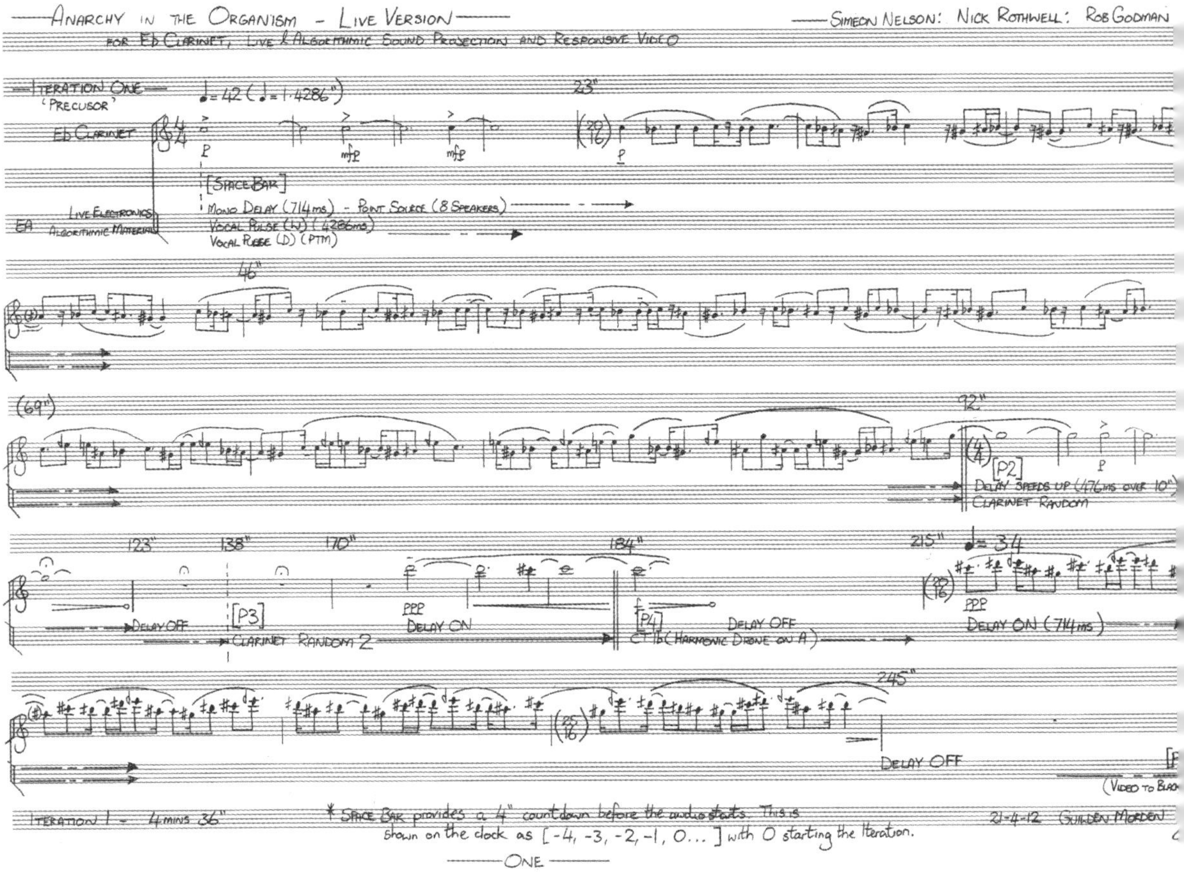

ABOVE Page one from the live version score, Rob Godman.

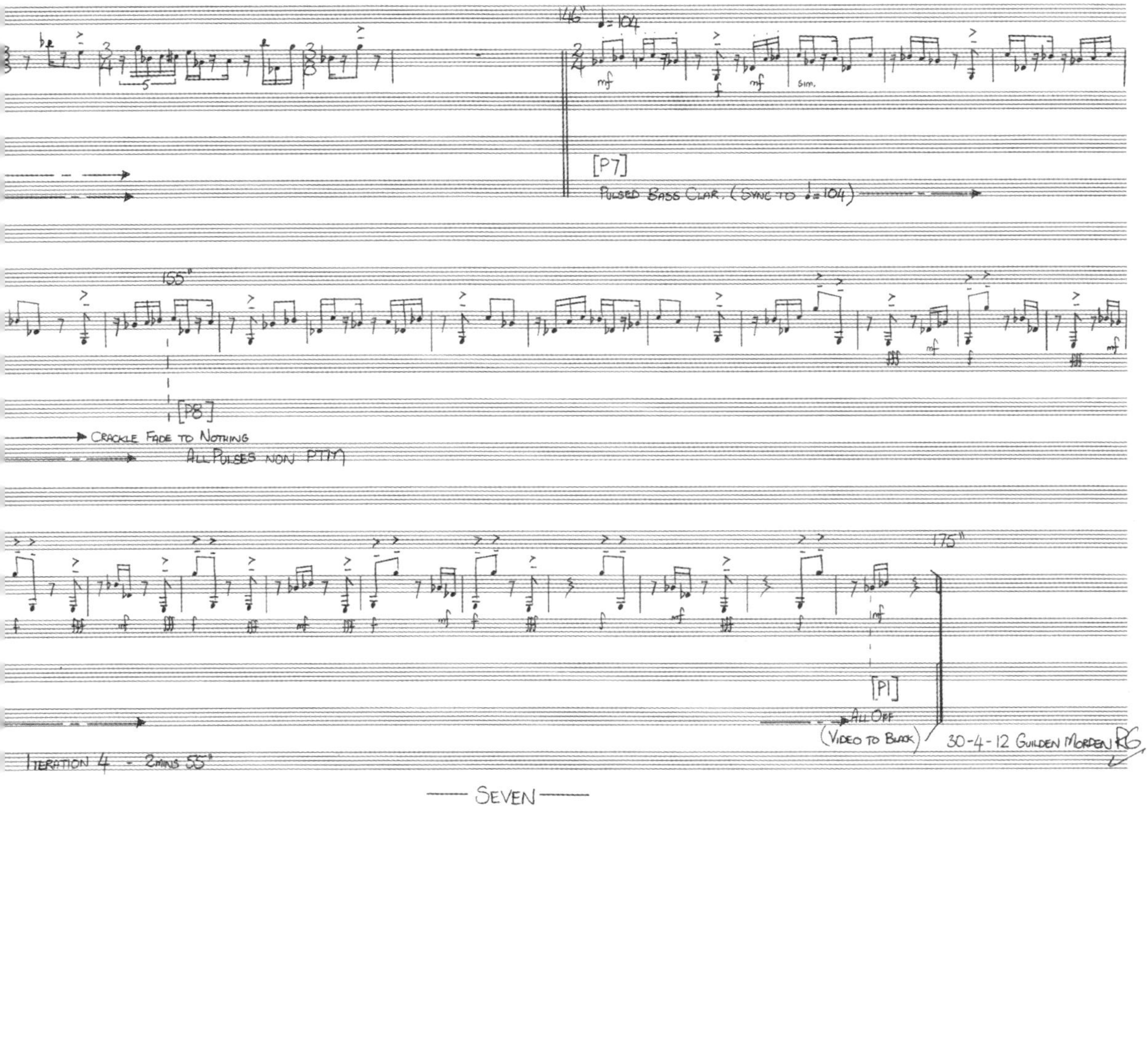

ABOVE Page seven from the live version score, Rob Godman.

(somewhat erroneously) Pulse Time Modulation (PTM)—the idea being that a repeating sound (a pulse) is subject to a constantly changing tempo creating a shifting accelerando/rallentando effect.

There are frequent examples of "spastic rhythm"—a terminology taken from Conlon Nancarrow's politically incorrect and rather offensive (even at the time Nancarrow adopted it) usage in his *Player Piano* pieces. In simple terms it implies a rhythmic inaccuracy, or to be more pertinent—a rhythmic pattern that disturbs a regular consonant rhythm (a 'limping' rhythm).

Where simultaneous multiple PTM's take place (possibly in combination with the spastic rhythm), any definitive pulse quickly becomes perceptually complex and/or chaotic. PTM attempts to mimic the cycles of life—functioning on the macro and microstructure of the work (in a pseudo-fractal fashion). Breathing, tension and relaxation, physical and psychological time all come under the auspices of the technique.

Acoustic space and the movement of sound in space has always been an integral part of my work as a composer. *Anarchy in the Organism* uses a technology known as convolution reverberation which is a very technical way of describing a technology allowing us to sample or record a real acoustic space. This means I am able to place sounds inside acoustics of specific buildings (which may have, for example, sacred or religious connotations). The spaces for *Anarchy in the Organism* include Chartres Notre Dame amongst others. I modelled early vocal works (by Perotin and Leonin) and applied various mechanical rhythmic techniques to them. The 'human' sound of the voices became dehumanised by the technology.

The live version of *Anarchy in the Organism* includes a clarinettist whose sound is processed and diffused using rhythmic techniques detailed. The performer provides an additional function of interrupter, interferer and disturber. We specifically chose the Eb clarinet as it has a highly focused and 'toy-like' (Romano) quality to its sound.

The fragility of tone also seemed suitable for our needs. When combined with the vocal material we discovered there was a close correlation in timbre. Kate Romano's playing and knowledge of the concepts behind *Anarchy in the Organism* were key to the development of the live version—without her passion for the work it would not have developed to the same degree.

The work carries a dedication to my Dad: for my Dad, who, towards the end of his life, claimed to understand what this was about. Whilst my Dad had been undergoing treatment for his condition, he spent some time hallucinating on a cocktail of post-surgery drugs about something he claimed to be "a show" which he believed I had presented in his ward at night. He eloquently described sounds coming from different places around him (multi-channel surround sound), images projected on walls and white smoke. My Dad had always had a very traditional approach to music but a great love for it all the same. However, he now firmly believed he understood what I did and thanked me enormously for putting "the show" on in his ward. It was clear that I would never convince him that "the show" didn't happen (and *Anarchy in the Organism* isn't modelled on it either)! Whilst the surgery extended his life for a year or so, we believe he had a close-to-death experience in which his perception of time and reality were completely distorted.

The live version was first performed by Kate Romano, Nick Rothwell and myself at the John Lill Music Centre, University of Hertfordshire on 15 May 2012.

Iteration One—Precursor 4'36"
Iteration Two—Fragile 2'05"
Iteration Three—Still 5'25"
Iteration Four—Redemption 2'55"

Approximate performance duration 16'00"

OVERLEAF *Anarchy in the Organism* —live version—Simeon Nelson, Nick Rothwell, Rob Godman (for Eb clarinet, Live & Algorithmic Sound Projection and Video). John Lill Music Centre, University of Hertfordshire, 15 May 2012. Clarinettist: Kate Romano.

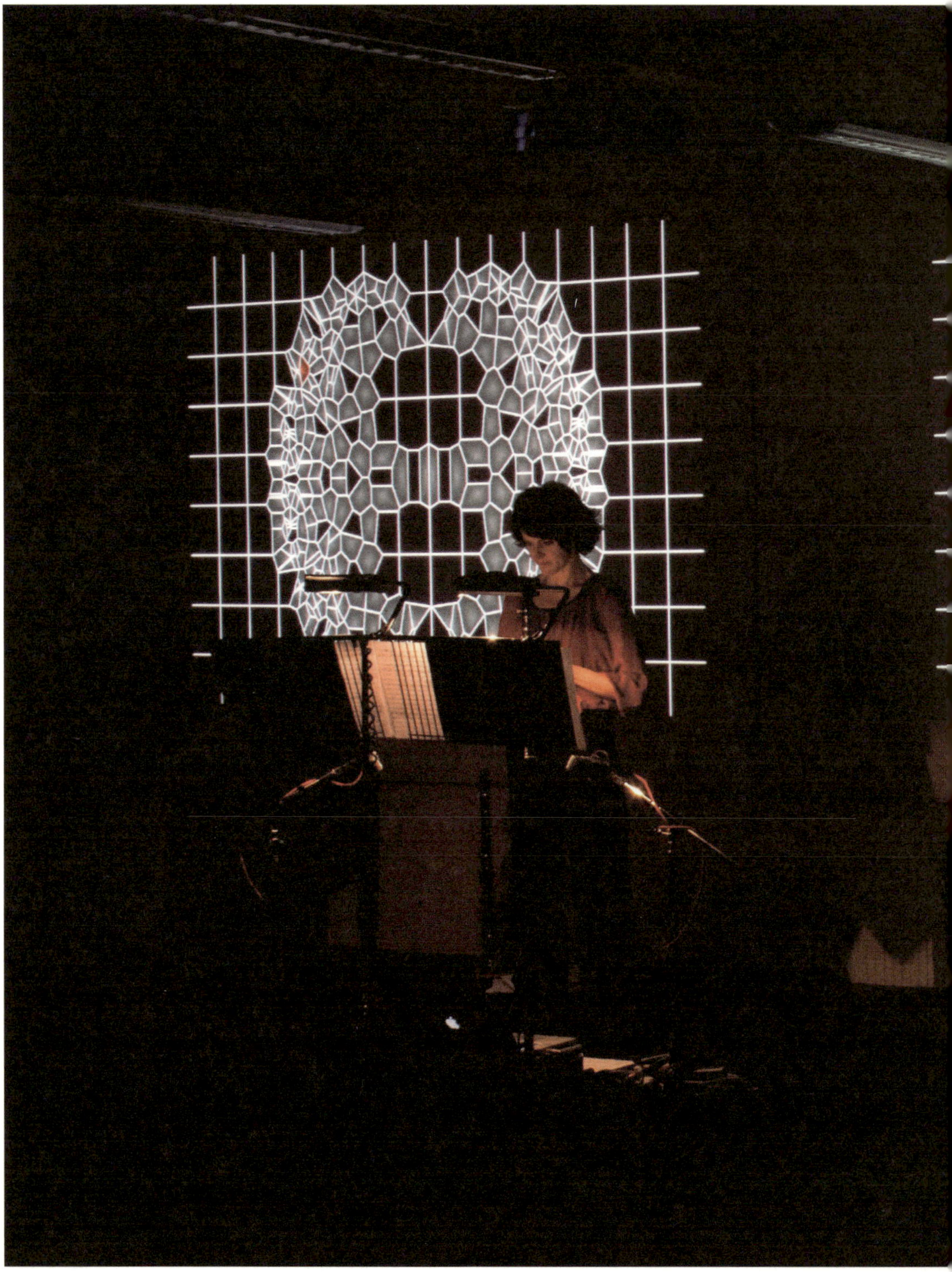

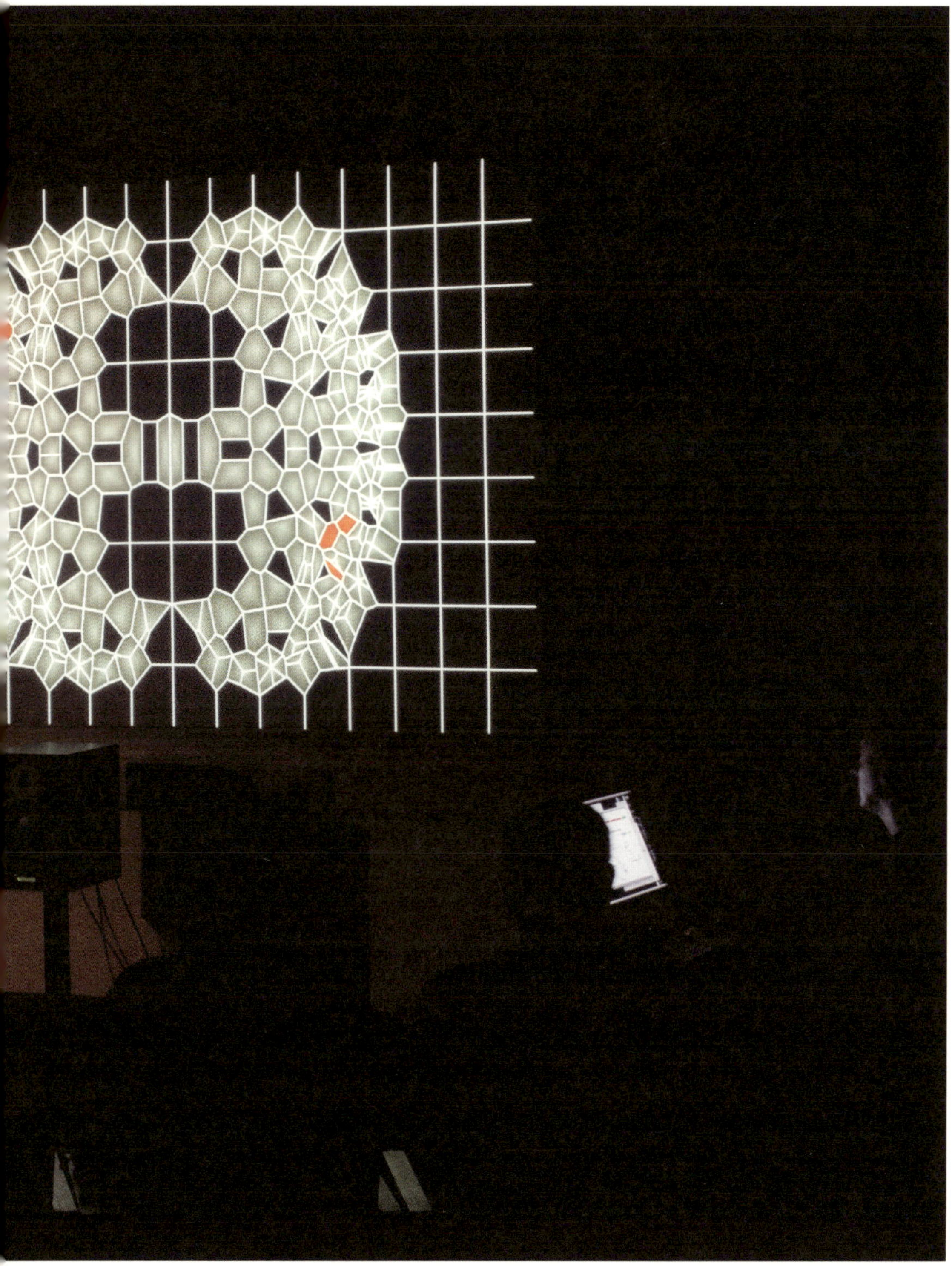

NOTES ON THE SOFTWARE

Nick Rothwell

I was approached by Simeon Nelson to construct the code and display system for *Anarchy in the Organism* after our previous collaboration, *Plenum*. Both works are concerned with modelling and visualising some aspect of the real, physical world. *Plenum* depicts fundamental forces of nature: attraction, repulsion, gravity and trajectory on both the microscopic and the cosmic scale. *Anarchy in the Organism* depicts growth, replication, corruption, subversion and recovery at the level of the organic body.

Computer-based art concerns itself with the balance between content and system: how much of the appearance of a work is exactly as intended by the artist, and how much is "accidental", the unintended

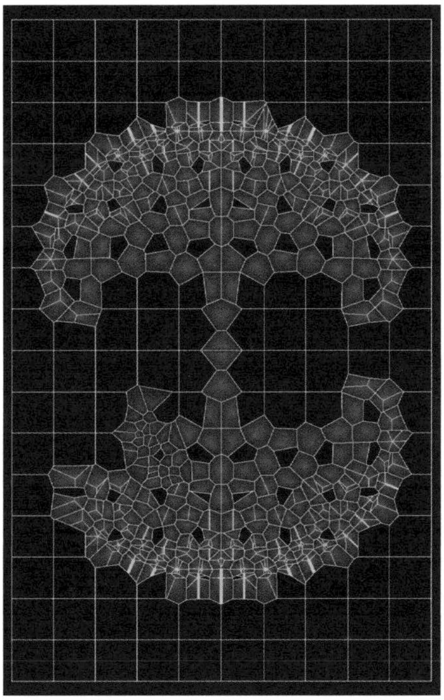

and unpredictable outcome of algorithms and processes set in motion by the construction of the underlying code. The design of the software is mediated by some sense of the predicted outcome, but at the same time early results or renderings feed back to influence the software's structure, either in terms of its fundamental form or how it can be controlled, parameterised and guided to yield the most aesthetically pleasing results.

Plenum was guided from the outset by concept images of the final result: a regular cartestian grid of points subject to various kinds of

ABOVE Screen shot of *Anarchy* video.

disruption and disconnection. (In that sense, there are clear parallels to *Anarchy*.) The final result bore close resemblance, at least in its early animation stages, to the result as initially imagined: the most obvious change was an inversion of colour from black-on-white to white-on-black (something which is hard to do in conventional artworks but instantaneous and trivially easy in computer art) for reasons of display quality. In fact, *Anarchy* was also video-inverted during its production for the same reason.

The starting point for *Anarchy in the Organism* was more concrete in its underlying concept—the exploration of the growth and treatment patterns for cancerous systems in the body—but less envisaged

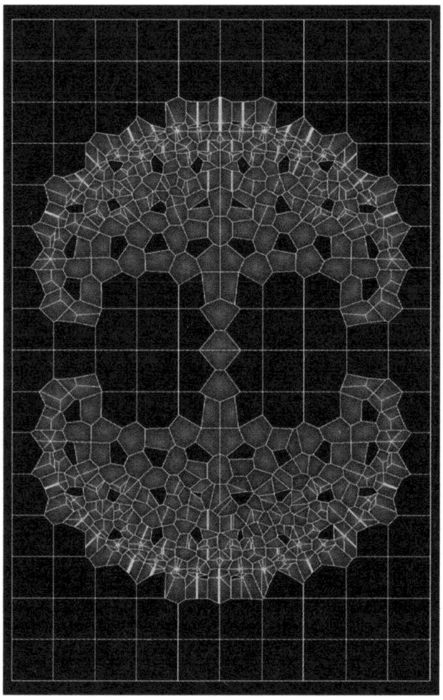

in terms of its final appearance. Organic systems are built through growth, and tend to have common properties of branching, scale and self-similarity: the blood vessels of a living body resemble the bronchi of the lungs, or the roots and branches of a tree. Some artificial structures also manifest tree-like structures due to their (human-mediated) growth: the streets and alleyways of a city, seen from above at sufficient distance, resemble blood vessels or branches. Major features split into newer, smaller copies which resemble the older ones except in scale.

ABOVE Screen shot of *Anarchy* video.

Initial illustrations of corporeal structures and city maps led to early software designs based around the generation of abstract, line-based tree forms. The application of Lindenmayer algorithms to simple initial data sets resulted in the generation of assorted tree-like forms, but we were limited by their primitive point-and-line structure: one of the appealing aesthetics of city maps is the dualism between the road system and the solid geometric areas which are defined by the roads which surround them—an appearance resembling two-dimensional images of cell structures, pertinent to the theme of the artwork. Eventually, an engineering shortcut suggested itself: use the branching points of the trees as seed points for a Voronoi tesselation,

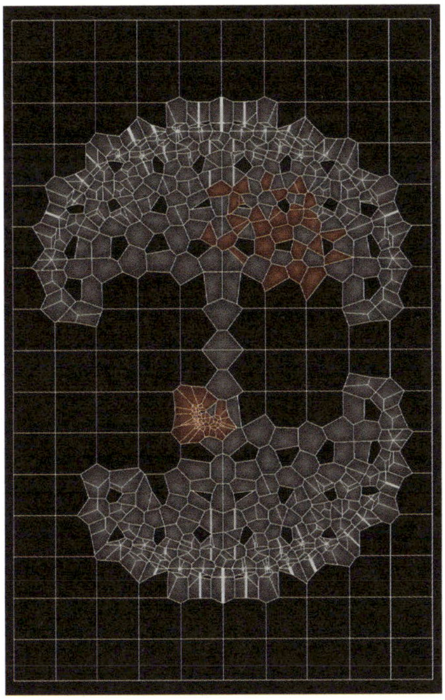

resulting in a plane of geometric regions with an organic, cell-like structure. The cells form a duality with the tree, and "growing" a tree from its root results in a cell-based growth animation which is both natural-looking and strangely intriguing.

From the start we were keen to model the growth and treatment of cancer cells in the animation system: for this, we needed some kind of underlying data structure which could be manipulated or corrupted in a way which reflected the behaviour of cancer, both in

ABOVE Screen shot of *Anarchy* video.

terms of its action on the structure and in terms of its visual effect. Simon Walker-Samuel provided example code of Lindenmayer systems imitating cancer growth, which we recoded in the animation system. When a cancerous system occurs in the animation, the "healthy" part of the tree shrinks geometrically, while a new "cancerous" tree is grown to replace it from the same point with a defective, mutated set of branching angles. In the Voronoi system, cells generated from the cancerous tree are highlighted in red rather than the default, neutral grey.

Fundamental properties of the animation—the tree depth, scaling, branching angles and position of the cancer growth point—can be independently varied to produce drastically different results. The artwork runs as a continuous sequence of rendering passes with different parameters, giving rise to a succession of distinct organic forms. In some, the cancerous systems are miniscule and hard to visually detect; in others, the cancer growth completely overwhelms the initial structure. This growth is reversible, representing treatment regimes: the mutated tree will generally shrink as the original is reinstated. The final phase of each animation pass removes the cells of the structure one by one, causing it to dissolve into an underlying cartesian grid representing its containing environment.

Anarchy in the Organism is hosted in Field, a live coding environment developed by OpenEndedGroup and designed for the construction of code-based digital art. The main algorithms of *Anarchy in the Organism* are programmed in Clojure, a variant of the programming language Lisp invented in 1958 and traditionally used for artificial intelligence research.

OPPOSITE Screen shot of *Anarchy* video.

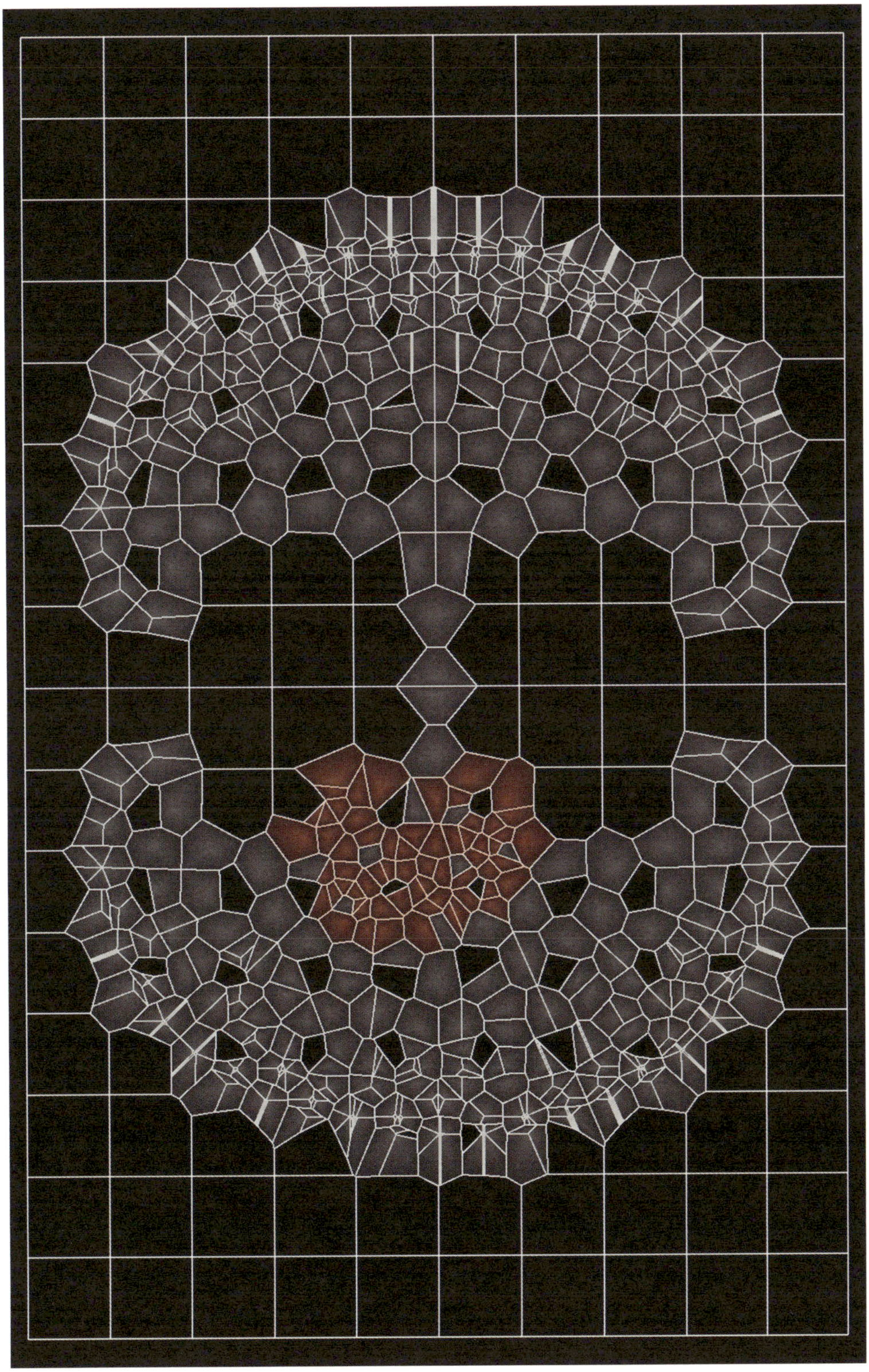

AUTHOR BIOGRAPHIES

Gilly Angell is a yoga teacher, shamanic healer and past life therapist with a London based practice. She also facilitates labyrinth workshops. At present she is writing a book on the joy of dying, the last art.

Monia Brizzi is a counselling psychologist registered with the British Psychological Society and Health and Care Professions Council. She practices at London Natural Health Centre and works with the British Association for Performing Arts Medicine and Society for Existential Analysis. Since 2006 she has collaborated with artists and curators as a consultant.

Jorge Castillo-Sepúlveda has a PhD in Social Psychology, Autonomous University of Barcelona. He is a member of Social Research Group of Science and Technology, GESCIT, and is Assistant Professor at University of Santiago de Chile. He works with socio-technical aspects of cancer informed by Science and Technology Studies.

Rob Godman is a composer, sound designer and programmer. He is interested in how sound behaves acoustically and has developed a number of techniques for controlling and building virtual spaces for use within live performance and installation. He regularly performs with the contemporary piano specialist Philip Mead and is Reader in Music at the University of Hertfordshire.

Simeon Nelson is a sculptor and new media artist. His interdisciplinary practice encompasses convergences between science, religion and art, complexity theory and relationships between art, architecture urban sites and the natural world. He is Professor of Sculpture at the University of Hertfordshire.

Guy Noble is Arts Curator at UCL Hospitals and is a trustee of London Arts and Health Forum. He has worked in arts in health since 1998. He has extensive experience in hospital arts programming and is interested in the role that cultural organisations can play in health.

Nick Rothwell is a composer, performer, software architect, programmer and sound artist. He has built software at Ballett Frankfurt and for Wayne McGregor|Random Dance, worked in digital media at STEIM (Amsterdam), CAMAC (Paris) and ZKM (Karlsruhe), and composed soundtracks for Shobana Jeyasingh Dance. He writes and teaches on music technology, coding and creativity.

Francisco Tirado is a professor in the Department of Social Psychology at Autonomous University of Barcelona, and founding member of the Social Research Group of Science and Technology, GESCIT. His research interests cover studies of science and technology, power relations and biopolitics and medicine.

Simon Walker-Samuel is a physicist at University College London. He develops novel medical imaging techniques to study tumour growth and development, and uses these images to mathematically model the delivery of drugs to tumours and to assess response to therapy.

Cancer is an autonomous (partly) system that has detached itself from the body regulatory system – it is a systemic failure – a crisis of auto-poeisis. It has escaped the pendulum pulse of the regulatory feedback systems of the body. It has fallen from the razors edge into chaos – complexity occurs at the boundary between order and chaos. Cancer is outside the functional zone – the fragile oscillation that characterises human life from sleeping and waking to the hearts pulse – to the birth death cycle. We are a single oscillation of this – our entire lives are as one intake and exhalation of breath. We are not substance – we are an event – from the subatomic patterns that hold our atoms together – we are a nested hierarchy of wholes within wholes. Is cancer the price we pay for the freedom to evolve into more complex forms with greater degrees of freedom and higher levels of consciousness?

The artist would like to thank:

The cancer patients who generously offered their experiences.

The patient carers and doctors.

The researchers who informed the scientific knowledge of the work.

A special thank you to Monia Brizzi for expanding and deepening the thinking and feeling behind the work.

Black Dog Publishing Limited
10A Acton Street
London
WC1X 9NG

t. +44 (0)207 713 5097
f. +44 (0)207 713 8682
e. info@blackdogonline.com

Designed by João Mota and Mónica Oliveira at Black Dog Publishing.

Cover pattern by Simeon Nelson, incorporating a screen shot by Nick Rothwell of the software prototyping for the artwork.

British Library Cataloguing-in-Publication Data.
A CIP record for this book is available from the British Library.

ISBN 978 1 908966 28 5

Black Dog Publishing is an environmentally responsible company. *Anarchy in the Organism* is printed on FSC accredited paper.

Supported by
wellcome trust

reuse recycle reduce

art design fashion
history photography
theory and things

black dog publishing
london uk

www.blackdogonline.com

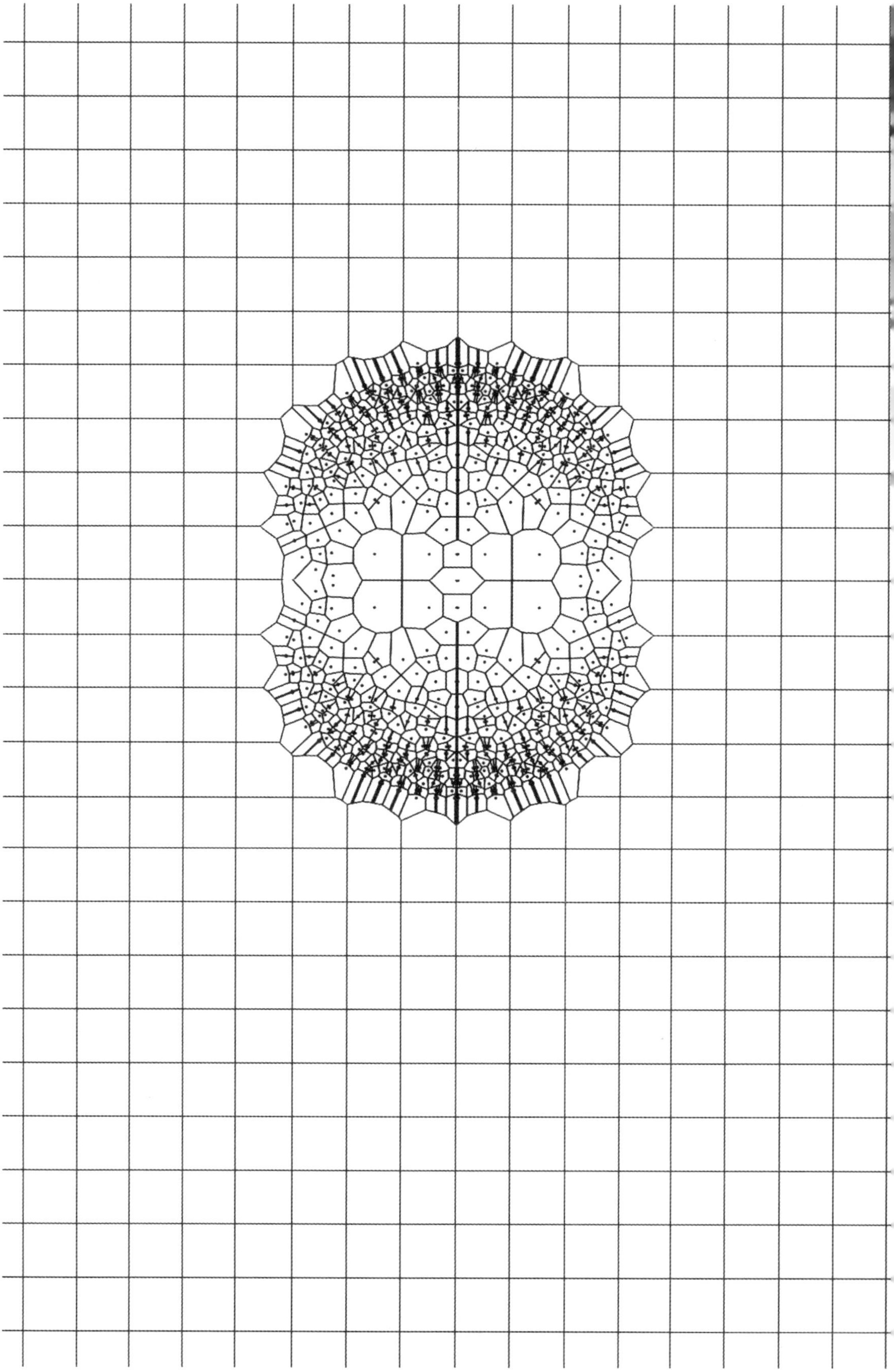